Teaching Teachers
to Use Technology

Teaching Teachers to Use Technology has been co-published
simultaneously as *Computers in the Schools*, Volume 23, Numbers 3/4
2006.

Monographic Separates from *Computers in the Schools*®

For additional information on these and other Haworth Press titles, including descriptions, tables of contents, reviews, and prices, use the QuickSearch catalog at http://www.HaworthPress.com.

Teaching Teachers to Use Technology, edited by D. LaMont Johnson, PhD, and Kulwadee Kongrith, PhD (Vol. 23, No. 3/4, 2006). *Teaching Teachers to Use Technology presents effective strategies for infusing technology into teacher education via the Millennium Project's PT3 program. This timely book includes models for professional and staff development, inquiry learning, network-based assessment, and collaborating through online learning and publications to increase the quality and quantity of educators entering the workforce as classroom teachers.*

Type II Uses of Technology in Education: Projects, Case Studies, and Software Applications, edited by Cleborne D. Maddux, PhD, and D. LaMont Johnson, PhD (Vol. 23, No. 1/2, 2006). *"Unlike many books on technology in education, this book avoids hype and anecdote. Instead it provides lucid analyses and research-based conclusions. It provides concrete illustrations of the way that technology provides new opportunities for powerful learning which were previously beyond our grasp." James Bosco, EdD, Professor Emeritus, Department of Educational Studies, Western Michigan University*

Classroom Integration of Type II Uses of Technology in Education, edited by Cleborne D. Maddux, PhD, and D. LaMont Johnson, PhD (Vol. 22, No. 3/4, 2005). *"Anyone interested in fulfilling the potential of instructional technology will benefit from this work. . . . Explores Type II technologies from the perspectives of a series of astute observers." (David Richard Moore, PhD, Assistant Professor, Educational Studies/Instructional Technology, Ohio University, Athens)*

Internet Applications of Type II Uses of Technology in Education, edited by Cleborne D. Maddux, PhD, and D. LaMont Johnson, PhD (Vol. 22, No. 1/2, 2005). *An overview of effective Type II teaching applications that use technology to develop new and better strategies for learning.*

Web-Based Learning in K-12 Classrooms: Opportunities and Challenges, edited by Jay Blanchard, PhD, and James Marshall, PhD (Vol. 21, No. 3/4, 2004). *Examines the possibilities of today's online learning applications across the K-12 curriculum.*

Integrating Information Technology into the Teacher Education Curriculum: Process and Products of Change, edited by Nancy Wentworth, PhD, Rodney Earle, PhD, and Michael L. Connell, PhD (Vol. 21, No. 1/2, 2004). *A powerful reference for teacher education departments striving to integrate new technologies into their curriculum and motivate their faculty to utilize them.*

Distance Education: What Works Well, edited by Michael Corry, PhD, and Chih-Hsuing Tu, PhD (Vol. 20, No. 3, 2003). *"A must read. . . . Provides a highly readable, practical, yet critical perspective into the design, delivery, and implementation of distance learning. . . . Examines issues faced by distance educators, offers valuable tactics culled from experience, and outlines strategies that have been key success factors for a wide variety of distance learning initiatives." (Veena Mahesh, PhD, Distance and Blended Learning Program Manager, Technology Manufacturing Group Training, Intel Corporation)*

Technology in Education: A Twenty-Year Retrospective, edited by D. LaMont Johnson, PhD, and Cleborne D. Maddux, PhD (Vol. 20, No. 1/2, 2003). *"Interesting, informative, relevant. . . . Having so many experts between the covers of one book was a treat. . . . I enjoyed reading this book!" (Susan W. Brown, PhD, Science/Math Methods Professor and Professional Curriculum Coordinator, New Mexico State University)*

Distance Education: Issues and Concerns, edited by Cleborne D. Maddux, PhD, Jacque Ewing-Taylor, MS, and D. LaMont Johnson, PhD (Vol. 19, No. 3/4, 2002). *Provides practical, research-based advice on distance education course design.*

Evaluation and Assessment in Educational Information Technology, edited by Leping Liu, PhD, D. LaMont Johnson, PhD, Cleborne D. Maddux, PhD, and Norma J. Henderson, MS (Vol. 18, No. 2/3 and 4, 2001). *Explores current trends, issues, strategies, and methods of evaluation and assessment in educational information technology.*

The Web in Higher Education: Assessing the Impact and Fulfilling the Potential, edited by
Cleborne D. Maddux, PhD, and D. LaMont Johnson, PhD (Vol. 17, No. 3/4 and Vol. 18, No. 1,
2001). *"I enthusiastically recommend this book to anyone new to Web-based program development.
I am certain that my project has moved along more rapidly because of what I learned from this
text. The chapter on designing online education courses helped to organize my programmatic
thinking. Another chapter did an outstanding job of debunking the myths regarding Web
learning." (Carol Swift, PhD, Associate Professor and Chair of the Department of Human
Development and Child Studies, Oakland University, Rochester, Michigan)*

Using Information Technology in Mathematics Education, edited by D. James Tooke, PhD, and
Norma Henderson, MS (Vol. 17, No. 1/2, 2001). *"Provides thought-provoking material on
several aspects and levels of mathematics education. The ideas presented will provide food for
thought for the reader, suggest new methods for the classroom, and give new ideas for further
research." (Charles E. Lamb, EdD, Professor, Mathematics Education, Department of Teaching,
Learning, and Culture, College of Education, Texas A&M University, College Station)*

Integration of Technology into the Classroom: Case Studies, edited by D. LaMont Johnson, PhD,
Cleborne D. Maddux, PhD, and Leping Liu, PhD (Vol. 16, No. 2/3/4, 2000). *Use these
fascinating case studies to understand why bringing information technology into your classroom
can make you a more effective teacher, and how to go about it!*

Information Technology in Educational Research and Statistics, edited by Leping Liu, PhD,
D. LaMont Johnson, PhD, and Cleborne D. Maddux, PhD (Vol. 15, No. 3/4, and Vol. 16, No. 1,
1999). *This important book focuses on creating new ideas for using educational technologies such as
the Internet, the World Wide Web and various software packages to further research and statistics.
You will explore on-going debates relating to the theory of research, research methodology, and
successful practices.* Information Technology in Educational Research and Statistics *also covers the
debate on what statistical procedures are appropriate for what kinds of research designs.*

Educational Computing in the Schools: Technology, Communication, and Literacy, edited by Jay
Blanchard, PhD (Vol. 15, No. 1, 1999). *Examines critical issues of technology, teaching, and learning
in three areas: access, communication, and literacy. You will discover new ideas and practices for
gaining access to and using technology in education from preschool through higher education.*

Logo: A Retrospective, edited by Cleborne D. Maddux, PhD, and D. LaMont Johnson, PhD (Vol. 14,
No. 1/2, 1997). *"This book–honest and optimistic–is a must for those interested in any aspect of
Logo: its history, the effects of its use, or its general role in education." (Dorothy M. Fitch, Logo
consultant, writer, and editor, Derry, New Hampshire)*

Using Technology in the Classroom, edited by D. LaMont Johnson, PhD, Cleborne D. Maddux,
PhD, and Leping Liu, MS (Vol. 13, No.1/2, 1997). *"A guide to teaching with technology that
emphasizes the advantages of transiting from teacher-directed learning to learner-centered
learning–a shift that can draw in even 'at-risk' kids." (Book News, Inc.)*

Multimedia and Megachange: New Roles for Educational Computing, edited by W. Michael Reed,
PhD, John K. Burton, PhD, and Min Liu, EdD (Vol. 10, No. 1/2/3/4, 1995). *"Describes and
analyzes issues and trends that might set research and development agenda for educators in the
near future." (Sci Tech Book News)*

Language Minority Students and Computers, edited by Christian J. Faltis, PhD, and Robert A.
DeVillar, PhD (Vol. 7, No. 1/2, 1990). *"Professionals in the field of language minority
education, including ESL and bilingual education, will cheer this collection of articles written by
highly respected, research-writers, along with computer technologists, and classroom
practitioners." (Journal of Computing in Teacher Education)*

Logo: Methods and Curriculum for Teachers, by Cleborne D. Maddux, PhD, and D. LaMont
Johnson, PhD (Supp #3, 1989). *"An excellent introduction to this programming language for
children." (Rena B. Lewis, Professor, College of Education, San Diego State University)*

Assessing the Impact of Computer-Based Instruction: A Review of Recent Research, by M. D.
Roblyer, PhD, W. H. Castine, PhD, and F. J. King, PhD (Vol. 5, No. 3/4, 1988).
*"A comprehensive and up-to-date review of the effects of computer applications on student
achievement and attitudes." (Measurements & Control)*

Educational Computing and Problem Solving, edited by W. Michael Reed, PhD, and John K.
Burton, PhD (Vol. 4, No. 3/4, 1988). *Here is everything that educators will need to know to use
computers to improve higher level skills such as problem solving and critical thinking.*

Teaching Teachers to Use Technology has been co-published simultaneously as *Computers in the Schools*, Volume 23, Numbers 3/4 2006.

The development, preparation, and publication of this work has been undertaken with great care. However, the publisher, employees, editors, and agents of The Haworth Press and all imprints of The Haworth Press, Inc., including The Haworth Medical Press® and Pharmaceutical Products Press®, are not responsible for any errors contained herein or for consequences that may ensue from use of materials or information contained in this work. With regard to case studies, identities and circumstances of individuals discussed herein have been changed to protect confidentiality. Any resemblance to actual persons, living or dead, is entirely coincidental.

The Haworth Press is committed to the dissemination of ideas and information according to the highest standards of intellectual freedom and the free exchange of ideas. Statements made and opinions expressed in this publication do not necessarily reflect the views of the Publisher, Directors, management, or staff of The Haworth Press, Inc., or an endorsement by them.

Cover design by Kerry E. Mack

Library of Congress Cataloging-in-Publication Data

Teaching teachers to use technology / D. LaMont Johnson, Kulwadee Kongrith, editors.
    p. cm.
    "Co-published simultaneously as Computers in the schools, Volume 23, numbers 3/4 2006."
    Includes bibliographical references and index.
    ISBN-13: 978-0-7890-3503-5 (hard cover : alk. paper)
    ISBN-10: 0-7890-3503-0 (hard cover : alk. paper)
    ISBN-13: 978-0-7890-3504-2 (soft cover : alk. paper)
    ISBN-10: 0-7890-3504-9 (soft cover : alk. paper)
    1. Educational technology–Study and teaching 2. Information technology–Study and teaching. 3. Teachers–Training of. I. Johnson, D. LaMont (Dee LaMont), 1939- II. Kongrith, Kulwadee. III. Computers in the schools. v. 23, no. 3/4.
    LB1028.3.T387 2006
    371.33071′1–dc22   2006020013

Teaching Teachers
to Use Technology

D. LaMont Johnson
Kulwadee Kongrith
Editors

Teaching Teachers to Use Technology has been co-published simultaneously as *Computers in the Schools*, Volume 23, Numbers 3/4 2006.

The Haworth Press, Inc.

New York • London • Victoria (AU)
www.HaworthPress.com

The HAWORTH PRESS _Inc._
Abstracting, Indexing & Outward Linking
PRINT _and_ ELECTRONIC BOOKS & JOURNALS

This section provides you with a list of major indexing & abstracting services and other tools for bibliographic access. That is to say, each service began covering this periodical during the the year noted in the right column. Most Websites which are listed below have indicated that they will either post, disseminate, compile, archive, cite or alert their own Website users with research-based content from this work. (This list is as current as the copyright date of this publication.)

Abstracting, Website/Indexing Coverage . . . . Year When Coverage Began

- *Academic Search Premier (EBSCO)*
  <http://www.epnet.com/academic/acasearchprem.asp> 2006

- *Advanced Polymers Abstracts (Cambridge Scientific Abstracts)*
  <http://www.csa.com> 2006

- *Aluminium Industry Abstracts (Cambridge Scientific Abstracts)*
  <http://www.csa.com> 2006

- *Australian Education Index (Australian Council for Educational Research) <http://www.acer.edu.au>* 2001

- *British Library Inside (The British Library)*
  <http://www.bl.uk/services/current/inside.html> 2006

- *Cabell's Directory of Publishing Opportunities in Educational Technology & Library Science <http://www.cabells.com>* 2006

- *Cambridge Scientific Abstracts (A leading publisher of scientific information in print journals, online databases, CD-ROM and via the Internet.) <http://www.csa.com>* 2006

- *Ceramic Abstracts (Cambridge Scientific Abstracts)*
  <http://www.csa.com> 2006

- *Communications & Mass Media Product Family (EBSCO)*
  <http://www.epnet.com/academic/comm&massmedia.asp> 2006

- *Composites Industry Abstracts (Cambridge Scientific Abstracts)*
  <http://www.csa.com> 2006

(continued)

(continued)

(continued)

Bibliographic Access

- *Cabell's Directory of Publishing Opportunities in Educational Curriculum and Methods <http://www.cabells.com/>*

- *Ulrich's Periodicals Directory: International Periodicals Information Since 1932 <http://www.Bowkerlink.com>*

Special Bibliographic Notes related to special journal issues
(separates) and indexing/abstracting:

- indexing/abstracting services in this list will also cover material in any "separate" that is co-published simultaneously with Haworth's special thematic journal issue or DocuSerial. Indexing/abstracting usually covers material at the article/chapter level.
- monographic co-editions are intended for either non-subscribers or libraries which intend to purchase a second copy for their circulating collections.
- monographic co-editions are reported to all jobbers/wholesalers/approval plans. The source journal is listed as the "series" to assist the prevention of duplicate purchasing in the same manner utilized for books-in-series.
- to facilitate user/access services all indexing/abstracting services are encouraged to utilize the co-indexing entry note indicated at the bottom of the first page of each article/chapter/contribution.
- this is intended to assist a library user of any reference tool (whether print, electronic, online, or CD-ROM) to locate the monographic version if the library has purchased this version but not a subscription to the source journal.
- individual articles/chapters in any Haworth publication are also available through the Haworth Document Delivery Service (HDDS).

As part of Haworth's continuing committment to better serve our library patrons, we are proud to be working with the following electronic services:

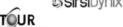

Teaching Teachers
to Use Technology

CONTENTS

ABOUT THE EDITORS

D. LaMont Johnson, PhD, Professor of Educational Technology in the College of Education at the University of Nevada, Reno (UNR), is a leading specialist in the area of educational computing and related technologies. He is the Founding Editor of *Computers in the Schools* and is Program Coordinator of the Information Technology in Education program at UNR. He has co-authored 10 books, including *Distance Education: Issues and Concerns* and the textbook *Educational Computing: Learning with Tomorrow's Technologies*, now in its third edition. A popular speaker and conference presenter, Dr. Johnson is active in several professional organizations concerned with advancing the use and understanding of educational technology

Kulwadee Kongrith, PhD, is Assistant Editor for *Computers in the Schools* since 2003. She received her doctorate in May 2006 with an emphasis in Information Technology in Education, College of Education, University of Nevada, Reno. Her research interests include the integration of technology in K-12, teacher education, instructional design, and program evaluation. In addition, she is interested in conducting her research on how technology could be effective in second language acquisition.

Rhonda Christensen
Gerald Knezek

Pathway for Preparing Tomorrow's Teachers to Infuse Technology

SUMMARY. The Millennium Project was funded by the U.S. Department of Education Preparing Tomorrow's Teachers to Use Technology (PT3) program for four years spanning 1999-2003. The project was led by the University of North Texas and sought to increase the quantity as well as quality of technology-infusing educators entering the workforce as classroom teachers. The Millennium Project succeeded in increasing the number of technology-integrating pre-service candidates from 20% to 80% of approximately 500 new teachers credentialed each year. Pre-post data gathered from key courses each semester verified that high quality teacher preparation practices were maintained while increases in volume took place. Data sharing with other PT3 projects helped form common grounds for discussion of similarities and differences during professional meetings and project-sharing collaborative exchanges. doi:10.1300/J025v23n03_01 *[Article copies available for a fee from The Haworth Document Delivery Service: 1-800-HAWORTH. E-mail*

RHONDA CHRISTENSEN is Research Scientist, Institute for the Integration of Technology into Teaching and Learning (IITTL), University of North Texas, Denton, TX 76203 (E-mail: Rhonda.Christensen@gmail.com).
GERALD KNEZEK is Professor of Technology and Cognition, University of North Texas, Denton, TX 76203 (E-mail: gknezek@gmail.com).

[Haworth co-indexing entry note]: "Pathway for Preparing Tomorrow's Teachers to Infuse Technology." Christensen, Rhonda, and Gerald Knezek. Co-published simultaneously in *Computers in the Schools* (The Haworth Press, Inc.) Vol. 23, No. 3/4, 2006, pp. 1-21; and: *Teaching Teachers to Use Technology* (ed: D. LaMont Johnson, and Kulwadee Kongrith) The Haworth Press, Inc., 2006, pp. 1-21. Single or multiple copies of this article are available for a fee from The Haworth Document Delivery Service [1-800-HAWORTH, 9:00 a.m. - 5:00 p.m. (EST). E-mail address: docdelivery@haworthpress.com].

Available online at http://cits.haworthpress.com
doi:10.1300/J025v23n03_01

1

address: <docdelivery@haworthpress.com> Website: <http://www.HaworthPress. com> © 2006 by The Haworth Press, Inc. All rights reserved.]

KEYWORDS. Teacher preparation, technology integration, evaluation practices, pre-service education

The Preparing Tomorrow's Teachers to Use Technology Program (PT3) of the United States Department of Education awarded $399 million between 1999 and 2001 toward the effort of producing five million new technology-infusing teachers for the United States (Carroll, 2005). In addition, corporations such as Intel invested extensive resources in this effort (Intel, 2005). Many projects have produced successful outcomes in terms of the numbers of new teachers, but a much smaller number have focused on measuring the new skills or strategies learned. The PT3 Capacity Building and Implementation projects directed by the University of North Texas quantified the new skills and strategies acquired by pre-service educators as well as the volume of new technology-integrating educators produced. The activities of these projects, their outcomes, and lessons learned from PT3 are the focus of this paper.

LITERATURE REVIEW

The National Center for Education Statistics (Jones, 2001) found that 99% of full-time, regular public school teachers have access to computers or the Internet in their schools. However, only one-third of these teachers reported being prepared to use computers and the Internet in their instruction. Shelton and Jones (1996) identified several key factors in the integration of technology into the school curriculum and educational instruction, one of which is teacher training. Since training is vital, it is important that pre-service teachers be prepared in the use of instructional technologies and learn how to effectively infuse technology into their instruction (Beyerbach, Walsh, & Vannatta, 2001; Clark, Martin, & Hall, 2000). The International Society for Technology in Education (ISTE) has developed a framework of technology goals for students and teachers through its National Educational Technology Standards (NETS) project (ISTE, 2001), and the foundation level of these has been adopted by the National Council for the Accreditation of

Teacher Education institutions for all students and teachers (NCATE, 2001). National educational organizations as well as society in general recognize the importance of computer literate students and technology-infusing teachers in producing tomorrow's productive citizens.

PROJECT MILLENNIUM OVERVIEW

Several initiatives were implemented at the University of North Texas in order to speed the adoption of model technology integration practices in existing pre-service teacher preparation courses. Among these were:

- Tech guides (UNT-resident undergraduate students from the Texas Academy of Math and Science) were hired to locate and organize Web-based resources for clusters of pre-service courses (mathematics, science, reading, social studies, special education).
- Technology Integration Fellows (doctoral candidates with years of K-12 teaching experience) worked on project activities as well as taught education courses.
- An organized Computer Education and Cognitive Systems class of pre-service educators (CECS 4800) went off campus to work in the schools for the purpose of providing technology infusion expertise (such as Web page construction) while experiencing successful teaching techniques in action.
- Pre-service students located educational software and Web-based classroom resources for partner district in-service teachers, as a class assignment in the Computers in the Classroom (CECS 4100) technology integration course.

In addition, technology-based enhancements—including: (a) posting syllabi and assignments online, (b) conducting all technology integration classes in computer classrooms, and (c) routinely gathering pre-post assessment data—were added to teacher preparation classes and implemented while technology facilities were being upgraded to serve faculty and students in teacher education.

Goals and Objectives

There were three main goals when the Millennium Project began in 1999. In 2002-2003 an additional goal was added. The four main goals of the project were:

1. To enhance technological knowledge and skills of future teachers so that they can infuse technology into learner-centered classrooms
2. To implement effective ways to address the digital divide across diverse populations
3. To prepare a new generation of technology-infusing teacher educators
4. To share common findings with other PT3 Implementation projects.

The Millennium Project consortium proposed implementing a total of seven pre-service teacher initiatives in the north Texas area. Technology-infusion activities were designed to continue the expansion of services to help meet educator preparation needs of the state and nation. One major emphasis for this four-year project was closing the digital divide, with the key areas of quantity, quality, and equity addressed in the preparation of technology competent and confident new teachers. Objectives in place at the beginning of the project were:

- Increasing the quality and quantity of pre-service technology integrating educators
- Expanding technology-infusing methods courses and instructor modeling of technology
- Providing technology-enriched assignments and assessment for special education pre-service teachers
- Establishing technology-enhanced academic content courses for pre-service teachers
- Establishing *fast track* credentialing for technology aides to be degreed teachers
- Developing Internet-based quality resources for pre-service teacher courses
- Recruiting new Millennium teacher educators from technology-infusing classroom teachers to work as Technology Integration Fellows in the project.

For the last year of the Millennium Project an additional goal (four) was added along with objectives to meet that goal. Those objectives were:

- Gathering pre-post data to compare changes in technology integration interventions for pre-service students at universities participating in PT3

- Comparing and contrasting findings across PT3 projects
- Reporting/disseminating findings to participants of the data-sharing activity and other interested constituencies.

Teacher Preparation Environment

The University of North Texas, seven K-12 school units, a community college, and two professional associations joined forces to implement project goals and objectives to achieve intended outcomes. The targeted outcome of the implementation phase (2000-2003) was to prepare 700 new technology-infusing educators over the three years of the project. This was perceived as an achievable outcome because the university and its partners had already been recipients of a one-year PT3 capacity building grant that allowed preparation for the implementation phase.

The activities of this project were managed by the Institute for the Integration of Technology into Teaching and Learning at the University of North Texas, housed within the Department of Technology and Cognition of the College of Education. The director of the Institute was the principal investigator of the PT3 grant, while an associate director was the technology integration coordinator for PT3 activities. An advisory committee composed of representatives of the K-12 partner schools and affiliated colleges met annually to provide feedback and discuss new directions for the project. In addition, PT3 project activity presentations were featured during College of Education faculty convocation luncheons at the beginning of six consecutive semesters during 2000-2003. These provided informal feedback opportunities directly from pre-service faculty.

Effectiveness of the project was assessed through multiple avenues, including quantitative pre-post data from classes, tracking of the types and numbers of classes infused with technology, interns placed in partner schools, and planning and needs assessment assistance provided to school districts at their request. Dissemination of findings was accomplished through presentations and journal articles. More than 30 dissemination pieces resulted from this project.

Instruments and Measurement

One strength of the project was the evaluation plan developed prior to implementation. Both an internal evaluator as well as an external evaluator were included in the project. Baseline data were gathered and faculty needs assessments were conducted. Well-validated instruments were used to assess both student and faculty technology-related indices. These instruments were later used with the data-sharing initiative to produce cross-project comparisons.

The following surveys were administered online to faculty and/or pre-service teachers:

- Demographic Items
- Needs Assessment
- Stages of Adoption of Technology (Stages)
- Teachers' Attitudes Toward Computers (TAC)
- CBAM Level of Use of Technology (CBAM-LoU)
- Technology Proficiency Self-Assessment (TPSA)
- Apple Classroom of Tomorrow (ACOT)-modified
- The Technology in Education Competency Survey (TECS)
- General Preparation Performance Profile (GP3).

Scales and Indices

Stages of Adoption (Christensen, 1997) is a self-assessment instrument of a teacher's level of adoption of technology, based on earlier work by Russell (1995). There are six possible stages in which educators rate themselves: Stage 1–Awareness, Stage 2–Learning the process, Stage 3–Understanding and application of the process, Stage 4–Familiarity and confidence, Stage 5–Adaptation to other contexts, and Stage 6–Creative application to new contexts.

The *Teachers' Attitudes Toward Computers* (TAC) (Christensen & Knezek, 2000a) measures attitudes toward computers in nine areas using a Likert scale of 1 = Strongly Disagree to 5 = Strongly Agree:

Interest–enjoyment and satisfaction in using computers
Comfort–lack of anxiety; comfortable using technology
Accommodation–acceptance of computers; willingness to learn
E-mail–usefulness of e-mail with students
Concern–fear that computers will have a negative impact on society
Utility–belief that computers are useful for productivity and instruction
Perception–overall feeling toward computers (Semantic Differential from 1 to 7)
Absorption–belief that computers are a part of many areas of work and leisure
Significance–belief that computers are important for student use

Level Of Use (Griffin & Christensen, 1999) is a self-assessment instrument adapted from the Concerns-Based Adoption Model (CBAM) Level of Use designations for adoption of an educational innovation (Hall et al., 1975). There are eight levels (coded for analysis as 1-8): 1–Level 0, Non-Use; 2–Level 1, Orientation; 3–Level 2, Preparation; 4–Level 3, Mechanical Use; 5–Level 4 A, Routine; 6–Level 4 B, Refinement; 7–Level 5, Integration; and 8–Level 6, Renewal.

The *Technology Proficiency Self-Assessment* instrument (TPSA) developed by Ropp (1999) was administered to determine the educators' self-efficacy (confidence in competence) for technology skills. Four of Ropp's measurement scales (with five items each) were included: E-mail, World Wide Web (WWW), Integrated Applications (IA), and Teaching with Technology (TT).

The *Apple Classroom of Tomorrow* (ACOT) instrument was developed by researchers at Apple Computer Inc. as a tool in a research project that spanned more than a decade (Dwyer, 1994). For the current project evaluation the descriptors for each of the levels was modified from the original version. Educators were asked to estimate their current level of understanding and use of technology. The levels include: ACOT1–Entry, ACOT2–Adoption, ACOT3–Adaptation, ACOT4–Appropriation, and ACOT5–Invention.

The *Technology in Education Competency Survey* (TECS), developed by Christensen (2001), is a self-assessment rating form covering teacher competencies in major areas addressed by the National Council for the Accreditation of Teacher Education (NCATE) standards. It is used to assess teacher education graduates' technology competency in six major areas: (a) Professional Productivity, (b) Project-Based Learning, (c) Problem Solving, (d) Assisting Students with Special Needs, (e) Teaching about Technology, and (f) the Ability to Use a Range of IT Learning Environments.

The *General Preparation Performance Profile* (GP3), developed by Knezek, Christensen, Morales, and Overall (2003), is an assessment tool for pre-service teachers based on national standards regarding their general preparation to use technology in the classroom. The survey was produced from the National Educational Technology Standards for Teachers (NETS•T) committee narrative for the General Preparation Profile for Prospective Teachers.

Targeted Activities and Outcomes

Goal One: To enhance technological knowledge and skills of future teachers so that they can infuse technology into learner-centered classrooms.

UNT technology integration foundation course. One objective of the Millennium Project under Goal One was to increase the percentage of technology-infusing teacher education graduates from 20% of the college population to 80% of the graduating college population. This goal was operationalized as having teacher preparation candidates complete the third course in the UNT technology integration sequence (Christensen & Knezek, 2000b), one which focused on using technology in the daily classroom learning experiences of children, as opposed to the first course on basic technology tools (word processing, spreadsheets, database, e-mail, Web access), or the second course on teacher productivity tools with technology (instructional design, PowerPoint presentations, interactive digital media, graphic displays, and laminations). The third course, called Computers in the Classroom (CECS 4100), focused on integrating appropriate technologies into the curriculum through the following topics: theories of learning, differentiating instruction with technology, creating Logo projects in MicroWorlds, developing Web pages, creating electronic publications, using digital cameras and other new information technologies in the classroom, curricular applications of concept-mapping software, integrating the Internet into instruction (WebQuests, searches, etc.), evaluating software, evaluating Internet Web sites, and developing a unit plan and portfolio on a chosen topic. The course was designed as a hands-on class and is taught in classrooms with workstations for every student. Outcomes were:

- During 2002-2003, 371 pre-service students completed the required Computers in the Classroom technology integration class through enrollment in one of 18 sections.
- When combined with several additional classes for secondary education majors that also contain strong technology-infusion components, the total annual production of technology-infusing teacher candidates exceeded 400. This number surpassed 80% of the approximately 500 new teachers certified upon graduation from UNT each year.

UNT College of Education professional education courses. Another objective of the Millennium Project under Goal One was to establish educator-modeled technology integration components in pre-service course curricula, in mathematics, reading, science, and social studies. Outcomes were:

- Strong technology infusion methodologies were adopted in reading early in the project and remained strong while mathematics gained strength in year two and has also remained strong
- Both of these disciplines (reading and mathematics) have woven the modeling of technology infusion practices into key courses taken by almost all teacher preparation candidates
- Science made gains in selected courses within the College of Education and within the College of Arts and Sciences
- Web sites were developed through the initiative that supported the curricula in mathematics, reading, science, social studies, and special education
- Many faculty were guided in developing their own course Web pages in which students could access information about the courses as well as resources related to the courses
- Faculty were also awarded tools with which to accomplish their goals, including laptops, digital cameras, handheld computers, and various software packages
- The initial goal of reaching 40 sections of pre-service courses during the grant funding period was exceeded.

College of Education courses for special populations. A third objective of the Millennium Project under Goal One was to develop multimedia modeling and assessment components within special education classes, and to introduce the product to 80% of all teacher preparation classes. One outcome was that the special education team created a library of technology-infused assignments for pre-service teachers majoring in special education. Also, the special education courses incorporated technology-enriched assignments to meet the needs of diverse learners.

Content courses in other UNT colleges. A fourth objective of the Millennium Project under Goal One was to incorporate teacher educator modeling of technology infusion techniques into classes in each of the UNT schools of Visual Arts, Music, and Arts and Sciences. The outcome was that collaboration in the School of Visual Arts proceeded rapidly and resulted in four courses revised to infuse technology among three participating faculty. In addition, the Arts and Sciences collaboration was successful in selected areas and resulted in course redesign in chemistry.

Goal Two: To implement effective ways to address the digital divide across diverse populations.

Paraprofessional credentialing programs. One objective of the Millennium Project under Goal Two was to introduce 25 new paraprofessionals per year to the *fast-track* program for certification and endorsement at University of North Texas. An outcome was the development of a Web site for advising these students into the program. A change in participating faculty priorities resulted in this objective being only partially met. Resources were redirected to a new goal on data sharing (see Goal Four) with approval of the PT3 personnel at the United States Department of Education.

Goal Three: To prepare a new generation of technology-infusing teacher educators.

Innovative learning resources. One objective of the Millennium Project under Goal Three was to collect and make available Web-based curriculum resources to serve the needs of the pre-service teacher educator and the graduating student teacher. The outcome was Project LIFT (Lesson Information for Teachers) which included 619 reviewed lesson plans available for both pre-service and in-service teachers. Difficulties in finding and funding qualified reviewers caused the project to be discontinued (due to lack of maintenance) when the lead faculty retired, approximately one year after the end of PT3 funding.

Another resource for teachers and pre-service students was an additional database developed for teacher topical resources. The students in the Computers in the Classroom course located resources for project partner teachers based on requested topics. These resources were also placed in a searchable database to share with partner school district teachers and pre-service teachers. The combination of these two databases exceeded 750 resources. However, local funding constraints have prohibited development of a well-maintained, user-friendly, renewal system or interface—both of which would be necessary to make this resource fully usable by area teachers.

New Millennium teacher educators. A second objective of the Millennium Project under Goal Three was to advance a cadre of Technology

Integration Fellows (doctoral candidates) to dissertation stage, thereby preparing these educators to take their place as model technology integrators among faculty of teacher education institutions throughout the United States.

The outcome was that 14 Technology Integration Fellows joined the PT3 Implementation grant team for the spring 2001 semester. Each fellow taught one course in a spring or summer semester, modeling technology integration to their students and requiring their students to use technology in class activities and assignments. In addition, each fellow worked 10 hours per week in a PT3-related capacity. This program capitalized on the rich pool of talent in the northern Texas area and brought master teachers into the doctoral fold at UNT. Table 1 lists the programs from which the doctoral candidates were drawn along with their grant-related duties.

End of grant indications were that this cadre of technology-integrating educators were doctoral students who were synergistic in their activities. In retrospect, based on numerous quantitative and qualitative indices, the data reconfirm that the Technology Integration Fellows were extremely successful in the Millennium Project. However, permission was granted to fund this initiative for only one year. Future opportunities of this type appear to be worth pursing.

Goal Four: To share common findings with other PT3 Implementation projects.

Data sharing for comparison of findings. One objective of the Millennium Project under Goal Four was to gather pre-post data to compare changes in technology integration interventions for pre-service students at universities participating in PT3.

Outcomes were that three universities participated in the first experimental implementation of data sharing in 2001, and after initiation four additional universities took part. This activity turned out to be manageable and perceived as useful to the participants. One indicator of success was that UNT, as well as universities in Nevada and Maine, continued to gather data on common instruments through spring 2003.

Another major outcome was that those universities who took part forged lasting bonds for collaborative comparisons that persisted beyond the end of the grant period. Those who took part were initially surprised to find that several different approaches produced very similar outcomes in pre-service educators, with fine gradations in differences strongly tied to local goals of the curriculum (see for example Christensen, Parker, &

TABLE 1. Programs of Doctoral Study for PT3 Technology Integration Fellows

Doctoral Program	PT3 Project Activity
Special Education	Locate and integrate technology into Gifted Education Coursework
Information Science	Locate and enter resources into Project LIFT Provide HTML instruction for project participants
Special Education	Assist with integrating technology assignments into EDSP 3500 (Individual Appraisal of Learning)
Curriculum and Instruction	Assist in writing the telecommunications and integration of new technologies chapters in the Curriculum Connections Guide
Educational Computing	Develop grant-related Flash modules Produce distance learning video for project activities
Early Childhood Education	Locate resources for human development/early childhood
Reading Education	Develop Web pages for reading education courses
Applied Technology & Training Development	Develop and maintain PT3 Web site Convert Instruments for Assessing Educator Progress in Technology Integration to HTML Develop Web pages for the Paraprofessional Summer II Institute Collect K-12 district data
Applied Technology & Training Development	Assist with distance learning in special education courses
Educational Computing	Work with teacher education faculty one-on-one to integrate technology
Educational Computing	Provide Web development and Listserv moderator support for project activities including the Technology Integration Fellows
Educational Computing	Liaison with Texas Woman's University PT3; Assist with grant reporting; Serve as the technology contact for mentors in collaborative rural school districts
Educational Computing	Organize PT3 Partners Forum hosted by a partner K-12 district
Early Childhood Education	Organize PT3 Partners Forum hosted by a partner K-12 district

Knezek, 2005). These findings produced interesting bases for conversation at PT3 Collaborative Exchanges and other PT3 meetings.

Disseminate findings. Another objective of the Millennium Project under Goal Four was to report/disseminate findings to participants of the data-sharing activity and other interested constituencies.

One outcome was that the data-sharing activities were a featured presentation at the PT3 project partners meeting in Washington, D.C., in the summer of 2001. The findings from these common instruments were also one of eight spotlight research papers featured at the National Educational Computing Conference in 2002. Common data findings were also one of rallying points leading to the creation of the new American Educational Research Association Special Interest Group on Technology as an Agent of Change in Teaching and Learning in 2002.

Indications of Systemic Change in Teacher Preparation Practice

Changes in practice. Several major changes in teacher preparation practice took place as a result of the PT3 grant. Among those were:

- The Computers in the Classroom course was added as a required course for all elementary education majors beginning fall 2001. The number of course sections (of approximately 25 students each) each year increased from six sections in 1999-2000 to 10 sections in 2000-2001, and to 14 sections for 2001-2002 (approximately 250 students). In 2002-2003 the number of sections further increased to 18, with 383 students completing the course.
- One assignment added to this course during the PT3 grant period was an authentic *Finding Thematic Resources for Teachers* activity. Pre-service students found Internet and software resources for classroom teachers based on their topic requests. This was very rewarding for both the pre-service students and our partner in-service teachers.

Assessment of impact. Evaluation data gathered over several semesters quantified the impact of the PT3 activities. Major findings are briefly described below.

Stages of adoption of technology. Pre-post data were gathered each semester from College of Education pre-service students. As shown in the first row of Table 2, fall 2001 stage of adoption gain was moderately large for CECS 4100 students, with an average effect size (ES) = .62. (Effect size is a standardized measure of gain calculated from (posttest mean-pretest mean)/pretest standard deviation.) Mean stage of adoption rose from 4.1, *Familiarity and Confidence: I am gaining a sense of confidence in using the computer for specific tasks. I am starting to feel comfortable using the computer*, to 4.86, approaching *Adaptation to other contexts: I think about the computer as a tool to help me and am no longer concerned about it as technology. I can use it in many applications and as an instructional aid.* The change in mean stage from 4.1 to 4.86 was highly significant ($t = 3.478$, 126 *df*, $p = .0007$). Effect size gains in stages of adoption for subsequent semesters of the PT3 project were in the range of .38 to .78, all of which surpass the ES = .3 guideline

TABLE 2. Pre-Post Technology Integration Measures for Multiple Semesters of CECS 4100 (Computers in Education) Students–Means and Effect Sizes

	Fall 2001			Spring 2002			Fall 2002			Spring 2003		
	Pre	Post	ES	Pre	Post	ES	Pre	Post	ES	Pre	Post	ES
Stages	4.10	4.86	.62	4.29	4.88	.53	4.45	4.81	.38	4.37	5.20	.78
TP-Email	4.07	4.45	.48	4.31	4.58	.41	4.36	4.63	.47	4.39	4.66	.46
TP-WWW	3.94	4.56	.86	4.13	4.46	.49	4.16	4.61	.82	4.12	4.64	.91
TP-IA	3.38	4.43	1.03	3.72	4.44	.85	3.66	4.47	1.06	3.64	4.80	1.08
TP-TT	3.39	4.46	1.41	3.78	4.27	.63	3.57	4.38	1.15	3.58	4.42	1.25

often used for assessing the point at which an impact achieves educational significance (Bialo & Sivin-Kachala, 1996). During the last semester of the grant, spring 2003 students rated the highest stage gain to date for CECS 4100; the effect of the course on student Stage of Adoption of Technology was ES = .78. This would be considered very near to a 'large effect' (ES = .8) according to the guidelines provided by Cohen (1969) for judging the magnitude of an educational intervention.

Technology self-efficacy. In addition to assessing Stage of Adoption of Technology as a direct measure of ability to integrate technology in the classroom, four other measures of technology self-efficacy (confidence in competence) were gathered. Mean values per semester for each of these measures gathered via the Technology Proficiency Self-Assessment (TPSA) (Ropp, 1999) are provided in Table 2. The TPSA measures confidence in four technology education skill areas: E-mail, WWW, Integrated Applications (IA) and Teaching with Technology (TT). Changes in the four measures for each semester are briefly summarized below.

- Results from fall 2001 were that effect sizes ranged from .48 for e-mail to 1.41 for Teaching with Technology (TPSA-TT). These values could be judged as moderate to very large gains in technology self-efficacy (Cohen, 1969).
- Spring 2002 results were that effect sizes ranged from .41 for e-mail to .85 for Integrated Applications (TPSA-IA), slightly lower overall than Fall 2001. Interestingly, this was the first semester that the course was offered after being announced as a requirement rather than an elective. All pre-service students in the

EC-8 teacher preparation programs were required to take the course following this spring semester.

- Fall 2002 analysis showed that effect sizes ranged from .47 for e-mail to 1.15 for Teaching with Technology (TPSA-TT). Students gained much confidence in their competence to teach with technology.
- For spring 2003 the students in this group gained on all TPSA indices. Effect sizes ranged from .46 for TPSA e-mail to 1.25 for Teaching with Technology (TPSA-TT). All gains for spring 2003 and previous semesters of the grant were statistically significant at the $p < .001$ level.

Discussion of technology integration course gains. Especially large gains were reported by the pre-service students enrolled in the technology integration course in the area of Teaching with Technology (TP-TT). Pre-post effect sizes were higher than 1.0 each semester data were gathered, with the exception of spring 2002. Highly significant ($p < .001$) gains also occurred in the primary technology integration measure, Stages of Adoption of Technology. These trends are visually represented in Figure 1.

Reconfirmation of trends through exit interview data. Data from exiting teacher education candidates were also gathered for analysis over multiple years. Surveys administered to exiting students included the Technology Proficiency Self-Assessment (TPSA), the Technology in Education Competency Survey (TECS) and the Stages of Adoption instrument. For each pre-service educator, this assessment took place roughly two years after the student had completed the technology integration class (CECS 4100). Results of analysis of exit interview data indicated that students felt better prepared to integrate technology in the classroom due to the changes made by the PT3 project.

Examples of Pre-Service Course Impact

Reading instructors at UNT took the early lead in incorporation of technologies such as e-mail exchanges, digital camera use, and Web page development. For example, the Assessment in Reading course utilized resources from PT3 funding since the beginning of the grant. Assessment of Reading is required for all pre-service teachers specializing in elementary education. Pre-service teachers assessed and tutored children each week. PowerPoint slides were created and a Web site was posted for the pre-service teachers' use. At the end of every semester,

FIGURE 1. Effect sizes (pre-post) for pre-service educators on five technology indices across four university semesters.

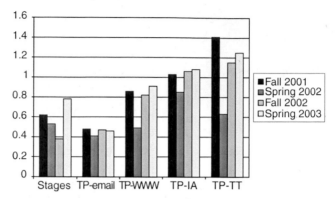

each pre-service teacher created a PowerPoint presentation of high-lights of his/her tutoring sessions. These presentations included digital pictures made by cameras purchased with PT3 funds. Areas of improvement (gains) made by the child were showcased. They included digital pictures of the participating child and pre-service teacher, literacy projects completed by the pre-service teacher and child, as well as other pertinent information. One slide was dedicated to what the pre-service students felt was the most successful activity in working with their child. More often than not, it was technology related.

Technology integration seminars were offered to teacher education faculty throughout the years of the grant. A survey went out to all faculty in teacher education as well as the College of Arts and Sciences, College of Music, and the School of Visual Arts in order to assess needs near the beginning of a semester. This process resulted in 15 seminars being conducted over the course of the grant.

One of the project's technology integration specialists worked one-on-one with teacher education faculty to integrate technology into their courses. This was deemed highly successful, based on reported progress and continuation of technology integration assignments in their courses.

A mini-grant competition was conducted after realizing that faculty needed to clearly articulate what they wanted to do with grant funds and follow up with presentations to our faculty as well as writing descriptions of their success stories. Three faculty were chosen to receive funding for technology tools as well as technology integration mentoring during the final semester of the grant.

A faculty technology proficiency assessment was given on multiple occasions during the grant to determine faculty competence as well as their needs from the grant. In 2001 the highest level of competence was in *I feel competent using e-mail to communicate with colleagues*, with a mean of 4.92 on a 5-point rating scale. The lowest rating was 3.38 on the item *I feel competent in recognizing when a student with special needs may benefit significantly by the use of adaptive technology.*

On the TPSA measures, the faculty reported an average skill level of 4.42 on TP-e-mail, 4.38 on TP-WWW, 4.09 on TP-Integrated Applications, and 4.04 on TP-Teaching with Technology. These measures were between the CECS 4100 students' semester pretest and posttest scores on the same measures.

An extensive pre-service education resource Web site (Teacher Tools http://www.coe.unt.edu/teachertools/) was developed by teacher education faculty to support PT3 efforts. The Web site is updated regularly and had been accessed more than 10,000 times by the end of the grant period. The Teacher Tools resource Web site has been extremely useful to other teacher education courses and continues to be developed and enhanced. This resource continues to be featured by the department.

Prospects for Sustainability

Teacher technology lab. Higher Education Assistance Funds (HEAF) were allocated by the college and the university as a match for the PT3 grant. Through these the Technology Teacher Lab was refurbished. The lab was equipped with 24 eMacs as well as an iBook cart with 20 laptop computers. These resources have been well utilized beyond the end of the grant. The lab is staffed 40 hours per week in addition to a technology education specialist overseeing the lab 20 hours per week. Faculty take their students into the lab on a regular basis as well as have students assigned to use the lab for software evaluation and other activities.

Required technology integration course. Due to the PT3 grant activities, the college program began requiring all students pursuing an EC-8 teaching certificate in teacher education to complete the Computers in the Classroom course (CECS 4100). This became part of all new degree plans as of fall 2002. The CECS 4100 course is now a prerequisite for two education courses.

Knowledgeable faculty. The knowledge and skills gained for teacher education faculty will continue to be evident in the classroom. Once the faculty were given resources and support, they embraced the opportunity to model and integrate the use of technology in their courses.

Continuation of partnerships and authentic assignments. While the assignment for 4100 students began as a bridge between partner schools and the pre-service students, it will continue and the students will continue to put their topical resources into the resources database that is a product of the PT3 project.

Special interest group at AERA. A special interest group (SIG) was approved by the American Educational Research Association that is related to the PT3 grantees. It is titled Technology as an Agent of Change in Teaching and Learning (TACTL). It was started by PT3 grantees as a means of sustaining the dissemination of the PT3 grant. Both the principal investigator and internal evaluator on this project were instrumental in the formation of the SIG and serve on its charter board of directors.

Continued collaboration with other PT3 project personnel. Collaborative grant proposals with other universities have been written to continue the "partner-like" relationships developed through the Collaborative Exchanges. For example, personnel from our PT3 grant at UNT are participating in the 2003-06 University of Nevada-Reno TITE-N project which was funded in the final round of PT3 grants. PT3 is believed to be the first large-scale program during the professional career of 21st century teacher educators that has encouraged colleges of education to collaborate with similar institutions across state borders.

Additional grants continuing. An Intel Pre-service Teach to the Future grant was received in 2001 as one of the pilot pre-service projects supported by Intel. Key personnel on the UNT PT3 grant are the co-PIs for the Intel grant. The program is closely aligned with the goals and objectives set forth in the PT3 grant led by UNT, and curriculum materials continue to be provided by Intel for teacher preparation courses.

LESSONS LEARNED

Many positive lessons worth repeating for others, and some lessons regarding avenues to be avoided in the future, were learned through the Millennium Project.

Faculty accountability. While many faculty appeared to be benefiting from the PT3 grant, there was no formal mechanism for them to report directly to the grant team. For the last year of the project *minigrants* were offered in which faculty had to apply to receive PT3 resources and services. Included in the *contract* was a required one- to two-page report on their activities. This turned out to be a much better way of accounting for faculty use of resources. In addition, the application process provided a clearly articulated plan for implementation for the faculty.

Building upon prior success. The broad foundation of initiatives implemented during the Millennium Implementation Project spanning 2000-2003 was practical due to the successful outcomes of the capacity building year (1999-2000). During the two stages of the grant period each of the following have been a success: tech guides, team teachers, new technology integration courses, and Web page support for pre-service teacher education. More than 30 scholarly papers and presentations were accepted from the project team. Mechanisms have been in place since 1999 to annually track trends in exiting student skill levels and in pre-service teacher education faculty self-reported skills. A mechanism to track and gather data online to establish community college graduates' bachelor's degree plans–with a track for pre-service teachers–was also created. The number of undergraduate technology integration course sections increased from three per year before the project began, to seven per year at the end of the capacity building grant, and further increased to 18 sections by the last funded year of the project. Our PT3 Implementation grant was awarded for 2000-2003 to continue and enhance the effective programs that were started with the capacity building grant of 1999-2000.

Planning for the future. For the 2005-2006 academic year, 25 course sections (of approximately 25 students each) were filled. The volume is approaching 100% of the undergraduate teacher preparation candidates within the UNT College of Education completing this technology integration course. Ongoing pre-post appraisal of teacher candidate skills has given us confidence that the high quality established during PT3 is being maintained through low student-to-teacher ratio, hands-on technology, face-to-face delivered courses. We note that the teacher preparation program at UNT received the distinction of being one of four finalists in the nation, for the award of Distinguished Programs in Teacher Education presented by the national Association of Teacher Educators (ATE), during 2004. We are confident that the technology integration initiatives established during PT3 played a contributory role. The pathways that began with this project appear to have become a conduit to technology-integrating classrooms of the future.

REFERENCES

Beyerbach, B. A., Walsh, C., & Vannatta, R. A. (2001). From teaching technology to using technology to enhance student learning: Preservice teachers' changing perceptions of technology infusion. *Journal of Technology and Teacher Education*, 9(1), 105-127.

Bialo, E. R., & Sivin-Kachala, J. (1996). The effectiveness of technology in schools: A summary of recent research. *School Library Media Quarterly*, 25(1), 51-57.

Carroll, T. (2005). *Integrated technologies, innovative learning: Insights from the PT3 program* (Forward). S. Rhine & M. Bailey (Eds.). Eugene, OR: ISTE.

Christensen, R. (1997). *Effect of technology integration education on the attitudes of teachers and their students*. Doctoral dissertation, University of North Texas. Retrieved from http://courseweb.tac.unt.edu/rhondac/

Christensen, R., & Knezek, G. (2000a). Internal consistency reliabilities for 14 computer attitude scales. *Journal of Technology and Teacher Education*, 8(4), 327-336.

Christensen, R., & Knezek, G. (2000b). Advancement of student technology integration skills through university pre-service coursework. *Proceedings of the 11th Society for Information Technology in Teacher Education (SITE) Conference* (pp. 1505-1520) San Diego, CA. Norfolk, VA: Association for the Advancement of Computing in Education.

Christensen, R. (2001). The Technology in Education Competency Survey (TECS): A self-appraisal instrument for NCATE standards. In J. Price, J. Willis, D. Willis, & N. Davis (Eds.), *Technology and teacher education annual 2001* (pp. 2290-2295). Charlottesville: Association for the Advancement of Computing in Education.

Christensen, R., Parker, D., & Knezek, G. (2005). Advances in preservice educator competence and confidence in technology integration: Comparative findings from two PT3 projects. In S. Rhine & M. Bailey (Eds.), *Integrated technologies, innovative learning: Insights from the PT3 program* (pp. 187-198). Eugene, OR: ISTE.

Clark, P., Martin, L., & Hall, V. (2000). Preparing preservice teachers to use computers effectively in elementary schools. *The Teacher Educator*, 36(2), 102-114.

Cohen, J. (1969). *Statistical power analysis for the behavioral sciences*. New York: Academic Press.

Dwyer, D. (1994). Apple classrooms of tomorrow: What we've learned. *Educational Leadership*, 51(7), 4-10.

Griffin, D., & Christensen, R. (1999). Concerns-Based Adoption Model levels of use of an innovation (CBAM-LoU). Adapted from Hall, Loucks, Rutherford, & Newlove (1975). Denton, TX: Institute for the Integration of Technology into Teaching and Learning.

Hall, G. E., Loucks, S. F., Rutherford, W. L., & Newlove, B. W. (1975). Levels of use of the innovation: A framework for analyzing innovation adoption. *Journal of Teacher Education*, 26(1), 52-56.

Intel Teach to the Future Preservice Program. (2005). Retrieved October 1, 2005, from http://www97.intel.com/education/teach/pre-service.htm

International Society for Technology in Education. (2001). *National educational technology standards*. Retrieved from http://www.iste.org/standards/index.html.

Jones, C. A. (2001). Tech support: Preparing teachers to use technology. *Principal Leadership, 1*(9), 35-39.

Knezek, G., Christensen, R., Morales, C., & Overall, T. (2003). GP3: An instrument for self-appraisal of general preparation in technology for prospective teachers. *Proceedings of the Society for Information Technology and Teacher Education (SITE) 14th International Conference*, (pp. 734-737). Albuquerque, NM. Norfolk, VA: Association for the Advancement of Computing in Education.

NCATE (National Council for the Accreditation of Teacher Education). Retrieved July, 2001 from Technology and Teacher Education at http://www.ncate.org/public/techcurrent.asp?ch=113

Ropp, M. M. (1999). Exploring individual characteristics associated with learning to use computers in pre-service teacher preparation. *Journal of Research on Computing in Education, 31*(4), 402-424.

Russell, A. L. (1995). Stages in learning new technology: Naïve adult email users. *Computers in Education, 25*(4), 173-178.

Shelton, M., & Jones, M. (1996). Staff development that works! A tale of four t's. *National Association of Secondary School Principals (NASSP) Bulletin, 80*(582), 99-105.

doi:10.1300/J025v23n03_01

E. Carol Beckett
Keith Wetzel
Ines Marquez Chisholm
Ron Zambo
Ray Buss
Helen Padgett
Mia Kim Williams
Mary Odom

Staff Development to Provide Intentional Language Teaching in Technology-Rich K-8 Multicultural Classrooms

E. CAROL BECKETT is Professor, College of Education, Arizona State University at the West campus, AZ 85351 (E-mail: ellen.beckett@asu.edu).
KEITH WETZEL is Associate Professor, College of Education, Arizona State University at the West campus (E-mail: k.wetzel@asu.edu).
INES MARQUEZ CHISHOLM is Professor, College of Education, Arizona State University at the West campus (E-mail: ines@asu.edu).
RON ZAMBO is Associate Professor, College of Education, Arizona State University at the West campus (E-mail: ron.zambo@asu.edu).
RAY BUSS is Assistant Dean and Associate Professor, College of Education, Arizona State University at the West campus (E-mail: ray.buss@asu.edu).
HELEN PADGETT is Adjunct Faculty, College of Education, Arizona State University at the West campus (E-mail: hpadgett@aol.com).
MIA KIM WILLIAMS is Lecturer and Doctoral Student, College of Education, Arizona State University at the West campus (E-mail: mia.williams@asu.edu).
MARY ODOM is Lecturer, College of Education, Arizona State University at the West campus (E-mail: mary.odom@asu.edu).
The research reported in this paper was based on a project funded by the U.S. Department of Education through Preparing Tomorrow's Teachers to Use Technology (PT3) Grant #P342A990351. The views and conclusions expressed are those of the authors and no endorsement by the U.S. Department of Education should be inferred.

[Haworth co-indexing entry note]: "Staff Development to Provide Intentional Language Teaching in Technology-Rich K-8 Multicultural Classrooms." Beckett, E. Carol et al. Co-published simultaneously in *Computers in the Schools* (The Haworth Press, Inc.) Vol. 23, No. 3/4, 2006, pp. 23-30; and: *Teaching Teachers to Use Technology* (ed: D. LaMont Johnson, and Kulwadee Kongrith) The Haworth Press, Inc., 2006, pp. 23-30. Single or multiple copies of this article are available for a fee from The Haworth Document Delivery Service [1-800-HAWORTH, 9:00 a.m. - 5:00 p.m. (EST). E-mail address: docdelivery@haworthpress.com].

Available online at http://cits.haworthpress.com
doi:10.1300/J025v23n03_02

SUMMARY. Teams of pre-service and in-service elementary teachers attended workshops, learned technology applications, and designed curricular units that incorporated technology during staff development accomplished through a Preparing Tomorrow's Teachers to Use Technology (PT3) U.S. Department of Education grant. Training focused on development of Units of Practice (UOP) with integration of technology, academic standards, and the ESL Standards for Pre-K-I2 Students (TESOL, 1997). Teacher teams infused strategies for culturally and linguistically diverse students to provide intentional language teaching for English language learners. Although the Practicum Plus Program was found to be effective, the authors noted difficulties encountered in recruiting participants. doi:10.1300/J025v23n03_02 *[Article copies available for a fee from The Haworth Document Delivery Service: 1-800-HAWORTH. E-mail address: <docdelivery@haworthpress.com> Website: <http://www.HaworthPress. com> © 2006 by The Haworth Press, Inc. All rights reserved.]*

KEYWORDS. Professional development, language teaching, technology integration, multicultural classrooms, pre- and in-service teachers, Practicum Plus Program

Teachers today recognize that pupils learn differently and have different strengths, abilities, and needs. For those acquiring English, there are also differences in native language, cultural heritage, social experiences, and prior learning. English language learners (ELLs) need an education that builds upon their strengths and acknowledges their differences while developing their English language proficiency. In addition, they need opportunities to develop computer literacy and the information technology skills that will prepare them for the increasingly technological job market in the new economy. The issue addressing effective education and computer literacy skills for English language learners has gained increasing importance with the passage of legislation that limits bilingual services in schools in several areas of the United States including Arizona, California, and Massachusetts.

During the summer of 2001 Arizona State University faculty addressed the issue of effective education for ELLs by providing teams of K-8 pre-service and in-service teachers professional development in technology integration into grade-level curriculum. The staff development was made possible by a Preparing Tomorrow's Teachers to Use Technology (PT3) Grant. Pre-service teachers were recruited from classes in the College of Teacher Education and Leadership; mentor teachers were recruited from local school districts having large populations of ELLs and in which pre-service teachers complete their required internship experiences. PT3 grant staff, Arizona Classrooms of Tomorrow Today (AZCOTT) teachers, and Arizona State University College of Teacher Education and Leadership faculty members conducted the Practicum Plus Program (PPP).

Through the PPP, pre-service and in-service teachers had opportunities to experience instructional applications of information technologies and learned to develop and implement an instructional Unit of Practice (UOP). A focal point of the program was integration of technology with multicultural and English-as-a-second-language instructional strategies. Integrating these two components enabled participants to provide optimal learning experiences that accommodated the rich cultural and linguistic diversity found in their classrooms.

The UOP is a framework for organizing content and embedding technology into teachers' classroom instruction. The seven specific elements of instruction, which comprise the UOP (i.e., Standards, Invitation, Situations, Interactions, Tasks, Tools, and Assessment) bring into focus and align curriculum with developmentally appropriate standards across grade levels and content. State and national academic standards provided the content focus, the six elements for technology integration in multicultural classrooms (Chisholm, 1998) provided a framework for multicultural technology use, while the ESL Stundards for Pre-K-12 Students (TESOL, 1997) provided the framework for language activities to promote English language acquisition to facilitate pupil success in school. Participants integrated the TESOL standards with instructional objectives that were formulated around academic standards. This integration fulfilled the intent of the TESOL standards, as they are not meant to stand alone but rather to serve as "a bridge to general education standards expected of all students" (TESOL, 1997, p. 2). The TESOL standards are important for teachers of English speakers of other languages (ESOL) "because they:

- articulate the English language development needs of ESOL learners,
- provide directions to educators on how to meet the needs of ESOL learners, and
- emphasize the central role of language in attainment of other standards" (TESOL, 1997, p. 2).

In the year 2000, immigrants accounted for 8.6 million school-age children in our schools (Camarota, 2001). There were 4.5 million school-age children who spoke a language other than English or who had difficulty speaking English in 2000 (National Association of Bilingual Education, 2001). Classrooms in the Southwest reflect this trend, with increasing numbers of pupils who do not understand or are not fully proficient in English. Including the TESOL standards in the training and development of the UOP addressed the need for incorporating intentional language teaching strategies into content lessons (e.g., social studies) for these pupils. It is imperative that culturally and linguistically diverse students have technology access and opportunities to use information technologies for authentic purposes involving problem solving and higher level thinking while learning English.

According to research on English language learners, integration of technology into instruction can augment positive self-concepts, promote English and native language proficiency, enhance motivation, stimulate positive attitudes toward learning, improve academic achievement, and foster higher level thinking skills (Diaz, 1984; Knox & Anderson-Inman, 2001; Meskill, Mossop, & Bates, 1998; Soska, 1994). Technology use, in conjunction with academic goals, allows students to take control of their own meaning-making and creates socially mediated literacy activities that foster the development of language and thinking (Meskill, Mossop, & Bates, 1998). When ELLs use technology in small groups, their verbal interactions enhance interpersonal and communication skills (Steinberg, 1992). Technology provides opportunities for cooperative learning which not only increase instructional effectiveness and efficiency, but also promote positive social interactions (Johnson, Johnson, & Stanne, 1986; Schlechter, 1990).

Technology-based activities can transform the classroom into a rich learning environment and prepare children who are ELLs for the technological world. Although information technology has a potentially positive effect on ELLs, teachers are central to the creation of a computer-enhanced learning environment that is learner-centered and motivating. Effective use of technology requires teachers to adopt new teaching models where technology becomes an integral component. ELLs, who are often among the disenfranchised and the computer-destitute, need teachers who can effectively integrate information technologies and the Internet into the learning process. Without such teachers these children's exposure to technology remains limited and inequitable.

Two questions formed the focus for data collection in the PT3 project. Question 1 asked: How effective was the Practicum Plus Program in preparing mentor teachers and their university practicum students to create a curriculum Unit Of Practice in their K-8 classrooms? Question 2 asked: How did mentor teachers and practicum students use the cohort listserve to support the community of learners?

There were 43 participants in two groups, 19 university students who were in the semester prior to student teaching (12) or completing their professional education preparation program as student teachers (7); and 24 in-service teachers, 19 of whom were supervising the participating interns/student teachers and 5 working on their own. The majority of students were in elementary education programs, including bilingual, ESL, and early childhood education. We recruited participants through advertising early in the spring semester, presentations in student courses, and at school faculty meetings.

The PT3 staff administered a 42-item, Likert-scale pre- and posttest questionnaire that assessed participants' beliefs and self-reported skill levels related to technology use and technology integration. For a full description of the questionnaire, see Zambo, Buss, and Wetzel (2001). The participants took the pretest on the first day of the workshops in the summer semester of 2001. They took the posttest on the last day of the workshops in the fall semester.

The researchers organized the questionnaire items in coherent sets in order to provide informative subscales that could be more readily analyzed. Subscales completed by both in-service and pre-service teachers included: general confidence in using technology, confidence in computer setup and general operation, confidence with software selection and use, confidence in addressing students with special needs, confidence in developing lessons with technology, beliefs about appropriate use of computers, and beliefs that computers are integral to classroom instruction.

The subscales that showed significant gains from pretest to posttest were those related to confidence in, or knowledge of, various factors associated with technology use. This finding strongly suggests that the workshops were effective in increasing teachers' confidence and skills in those targeted areas. Those subscales that were already high in the pretest did not increase. Nor were there any significant changes found in the beliefs subscales. This finding is an indication that the students and teachers who participated in the workshops came with a predisposition favoring educational technology.

Participants also cooperated in online discussions through Blackboard, an online course management tool. The three purposes of the discussion board were to provide the participants with skills of electronic communication, to encourage collegial sharing, and to create a community of learners who could interact beyond the time and place of the actual workshops.

Participants consistently used the discussion board to share teaching ideas and resources, to reflect and discuss activities that occurred during the workshops, and to stay abreast of current events that could affect their classrooms. They also shared information about Web sites and on how to complete workshop assignments. In addition, they communicated ideas about integrating technology in the classroom.

All pre-service and in-service teacher teams, and all individuals working alone, prepared and implemented Units of Practice that integrated technology into the curriculum. PT3 personnel used a rubric to evaluate and identify proficiency levels for each component of the UOP. The PT3 staff evaluated each component on a range of Accomplished, Developing, or Emerging (http://newali.apple.com/ali_media/Users/144/files/others/UOP_RUBRIC.pdf). Results indicated that most participants had strengths in the Invitations, Tasks, Interactions, and Situations components. Several participants also achieved the Accomplished level in the standards components including the TESOL standards for English acquisition by bilingual and ESL teams. Faculty and evaluators felt the proficiency level achieved in the TESOL standards showed the pre-service and in-service teachers' desire to provide content area instruction that supports English language development.

In this model of teacher preparation, most of the staff development activities in technology integration were held during the summer. In the semester following the summer training, the pre-service student helped the in-service teacher implement the technology-rich unit created in the workshops in his/her practicum classroom. In-service teachers and pre-service teachers indicated that they appreciated the opportunity to work together prior to the practicum experience. They were able to establish a trust between them as they increased their knowledge of hardware and software. They also expressed an increase in confidence in their ability to design and implement technology in the curriculum. The inclusion of the TESOL standards helped them to meet the needs of the English language learners in the classrooms.

Although this model of professional development was effective, there were some difficulties. It was not easy to locate and match mentor teachers with students for the early summer course before the practicum semester. There needed to be a closer working relationship with the College of Teacher Education and Leadership Field Placement Office prior to design of the summer program. If the problems involved with creating the mentor and student teacher pairs can be resolved, this program model is promising.

In conclusion, it was gratifying to find that all participants included appropriate standards and technology integration and applications in developing their UOP. The inclusion of TESOL standards for intentional language teaching not only addressed the obvious need of English language learners but also incidentally provided for language development for all students. Pre-service teachers and in-service teachers used the discussion board effectively as a communication tool to improve their use of technology in the classroom. The only aspect of the workshops that posed a problem was recruitment of participants. The authors believe that creating a more flexible schedule to accommodate pre-service and in-service teachers' routines and responsibilities could increase the numbers of participants.

REFERENCES

Camarota, S. A. (2001). *Immigrants in the United States-2000: A snapshot of America's foreign-born population.* Center for Immigration Studies. Retrieved January 28, 2003, from http://www.cis.org/articles/2001/back101.html

Chisholm, I. M. (1998). Six elements for technology integration in multicultural classrooms. *Journal of Information Technology for Teacher Education, 7*(2), 247-268.

Diaz, S. (1984, November). *Bilingual-bicultural computer experts: Traditional literacy through computer literacy.* Paper presented at the meeting of the American Anthropological Association, Denver, CO.

Johnson, R., Johnson, D., & Stanne, M. (1986). Comparison of computer-assisted, competitive and individualistic learning. *American Educational Research Journal, 23*(3), 382-392.

Knox, C., & Anderson-Inman, L. (2001). Migrant ESL high school students succeed using networked laptops. *Learning and Leading with Technology, 28*(5), 18-21, 52-53.

Meskill, C., Mossop, J., & Bates, R. (1998, April). *Electronic texts and learners of English as a second language.* Paper presented at the annual meeting of the American Educational Research Association, San Diego, CA. (ERIC Document Reproduction Service No. ED436965)

National Association for Bilingual Education. (2001). *NABE statement on president's 2004 budget proposal.* Retrieved March 24, 2003, from http://www.nabe.org/press_feaure.asp

Schlechter, T. (1990). The relative instructional efficiency of small group computer-based telecommunications for instruction. *Journal of Computer-Based Instruction, 6*(3), 329-341.

Soska, M. (1994). Educational technology enhances the LEP classroom. *Forum, 17*(5). Retrieved January 1, 2003, from http://www.ncbe.gwu.edu/ncbepubs/forurn/1705.htrn

Steinberg, E. R. (1992). The potential of computer-based telecommunications for instruction. *Journal of Computer-Based Instruction, 19*(2), 42-46.

Teachers of English to Speakers of Other Languages (1997). *ESL standards for pre-K-12 students*. Alexandria, VA: Author.

Zambo, R., Buss, R. R., & Wetzel, K. (2001). Technology integration in K-12 classrooms: Evaluating teachers' dispositions, knowledge, and abilities. *Technology and Teacher Education Annual: Proceedings from the Twelfth Annual Conference of the Society for Technology and Teacher Education* (pp. 2165-2169). Charlottesville, VA: Association for the Advancement of Computing in Education.

doi:10.1300/J025v23n03_02

Mesut Duran
Paul R. Fossum
Gail R. Luera

Technology and Pedagogical Renewal: Conceptualizing Technology Integration into Teacher Preparation

SUMMARY. Research indicates that, if future teachers are to effectively use technology, their pre-service preparation should employ multiple components. These components include core course work in educational technology, faculty modeling, and clinical experiences. This paper describes and analyzes one model for drawing these three

MESUT DURAN is Assistant Professor of Educational Technology, The University of Michigan-Dearborn, School of Education, Dearborn, MI 48129-1491 (E-mail: mduran@umich.edu).
PAUL R. FOSSUM is Assistant Professor of Education Foundations, School of Education, University of Michigan-Dearborn, Dearborn, MI 48129-1491 (E-mail: pfossum@umich.edu).
GAIL R. LUERA is Assistant Professor of Technologies and Science Education, School of Education, University of Michigan-Dearborn, Dearborn, MI 48129-1491 (E-mail: grl@umd.umich.edu).

The research reported in this article was based on a project funded by the U.S. Department of Education through Preparing Tomorrow's Teachers to use Technology (PT3) Grant# P342A010073. The views and conclusions expressed are those of the authors, and no endorsement by the U.S. Department of Education should be inferred.

[Haworth co-indexing entry note]: "Technology and Pedagogical Renewal: Conceptualizing Technology Integration into Teacher Preparation." Duran, Mesut, Paul R. Fossum, and Gail R. Luera. Co-published simultaneously in *Computers in the Schools* (The Haworth Press, Inc.) Vol. 23, No. 3/4, 2006, pp. 31-54; and: *Teaching Teachers to Use Technology* (ed: D. LaMont Johnson, and Kulwadee Kongrith) The Haworth Press, Inc., 2006, pp. 31-54. Single or multiple copies of this article are available for a fee from The Haworth Document Delivery Service [1-800-HAWORTH, 9:00 a.m. - 5:00 p.m. (EST). E-mail address: docdelivery@haworthpress.com].

31

components coherently together in a teacher preparation program. The paper further reports on a research project that applies this model at a major Midwest research university. In the conclusion section the paper identifies and discusses ways in which the model presented responds effectively to the need for a comprehensive program for preparing a technology-proficient teaching force. doi:10.1300/J025v23n03_03 *[Article copies available for a fee from The Haworth Document Delivery Service: 1-800-HAWORTH. E-mail address: <docdelivery@haworthpress.com> Website: <http://www.HaworthPress.com> © 2006 by The Haworth Press, Inc. All rights reserved.]*

KEYWORDS. Teacher education, professional development, university/school collaboration, learning communities, educational change, education renewal, educational standards, instructional technology, technology integration, computers in education

A considerable amount of research on educational technology suggests that preparing technologically proficient educators relies on multiple components. Basic instruction in an educational computing course–preferably near the beginning of the professional sequence of classes–plays an important role in introducing pre-service teachers to fundamental technology concepts and skills (Kim & Peterson, 1992). Yet such course work is not sufficient in creating technology-proficient teachers (Hunt, 1994; Moursund & Bielefeldt, 1999; Wetzel, 1993). An additional important element in the preparation of a technology-proficient teacher is the opportunity to observe technology-proficient faculty, modeling effective use of technology in methods and content courses (O'Bannon, Matthew, & Thomas, 1998; Moursund & Bielefeldt, 1999; Strudler & Wetzel, 1999). Scholarship in the field of educational technology has also indicated that effective preparation of technology-proficient teachers calls for the meaningful integration of advanced technology into the pre-service teacher's field experiences (Gunn, 1991; Novak & Berger, 1991; Wetzel & McLean, 1997; Wepner & Mobley, 1998).

These three elements, then, contribute to the comprehensive preparation of technology-proficient educators–core course work, effective faculty modeling of instructional technology, and technology-enriched field experiences (Duran 2000; Instructional Technology Resource Center [ITRC], 1998; Moursund & Bielefeldt, 1999; National Council for Accreditation of Teacher Education [NCATE], 1997). Yet while a large and growing proportion of the nation's postsecondary teacher preparation institutions require core course work in educational technology (Vagle, 1995), the typical teacher education program does not include sustained faculty modeling nor does it provide field experiences that meaningfully integrate educational technology (Duran 2000; Moursund & Bielefeldt, 1999).

There is a pressing need for models that address all of these three components, and that foster progress toward the end goal of producing a technology-proficient teaching force. This paper first describes and analyzes one model for change called the Michigan Teachers' Technology Education Network or "MITTEN." The model envisions a three-year process aimed at aligning and strengthening the three vital elements identified above–core coursework, faculty modeling, and technology-enriched field experiences–thus helping to encourage the sound use of advanced technology tools in the region's schools. The discussion in this section links the model with the literature on instructional technology in particular. Further, because Wilburg (1997) has maintained that "efforts to integrate technology with teaching must consider the research on change" (p. 174), the discussion also includes considerable reference to theoretical and conceptual literature on educational change in general. Second, the paper reports on the MITTEN project's findings from the first three cohort groups who participated in the study from September 1, 2001 through April 30, 2003. Third, in a concluding section, the paper describes ways in which the model presented responds to the need for a comprehensive program for preparing technology-proficient future teachers.

A MODEL IN THEORETICAL PERSPECTIVE

Various parties are involved in the work of preparing future teachers, and these include, most obviously, postsecondary schools of education. Commonly, such teacher education units maintain tight links with K-12 schools in their regions to serve as sites within which future teachers pursue coordinated clinical experiences. In addition to the schools of education and their K-12 partners, colleges of arts and sciences have vital roles: Within these units in particular, future teachers shape their expertise in various fields of emphasis. The task of integrating the components discussed above–core course work in educational technology, faculty modeling, and clinical experience–warrants the co-operative engagement of all of these entities.

MITTEN and the Educational Change Context: Descriptive and Analytic Overview

In responding to PT3's (Preparing Tomorrows' Teachers to Use Technology) call for sustained and meaningful linkages between the P-12 and the postsecondary sectors, the MITTEN project discussed here has adopted a model similar to John Goodlad's (1994) "centers of pedagogy" (see Figure 1). Like the Holmes Group (1995) vision of professional development schools as venues for sustained discourse around the young teacher's practice, Goodlad's centers of pedagogy call for new and stronger relationships between P-12 and postsecondary institutions. The MITTEN project, based in the University of Michigan Dearborn's School of Education, involves UM-D's College of Arts, Sciences, and Letters and nearby Henry Ford Community College as additional higher education collaborators that are engaged in the work of teacher preparation. Several local P-12 institutions, which sponsor UM-D's pre-service teachers for their clinical experiences, are also engaged in the project.

As Figure 1 illustrates, Goodlad's contention is that effective interaction regarding teaching improvement calls for engagement among three entities: schools of education, school districts, and colleges of arts and sciences. Certainly, while each of these three participants has its own

FIGURE 1. John I. Goodlad's (1994) depiction of the "Major Collaborators in a Center of Pedagogy" (p. 9). Reprinted with permission.

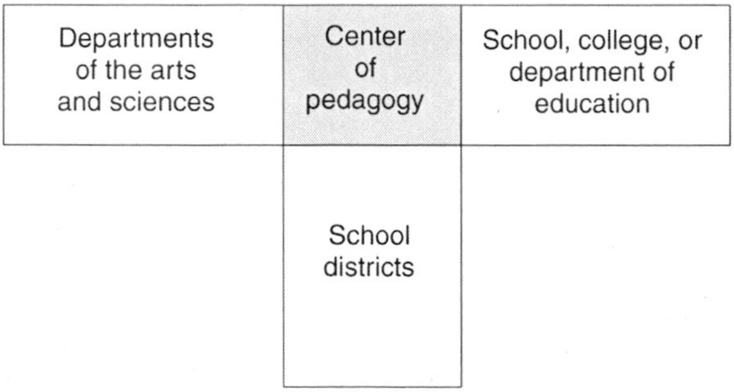

Departments of the arts and sciences	Center of pedagogy	School, college, or department of education
	School districts	

functions and other business to attend to, Goodlad (1994) has stressed that each is an essential and equal player in a healthy teacher preparation "ecosystem" (p. 9). More than just a setting, then, the center of pedagogy "brings together simultaneously and integratively the commonly scattered pieces of the teacher education enterprise and embeds them in reflective attention to the art and science of teaching" (Goodlad, 1994, p. 10). In sum, centers of pedagogy constitute a means of addressing the shortcomings of the status quo in teacher education, comprised, as it normally is, of an "undergraduate curriculum of general and special studies interspersed with essentially required courses in education and student teaching" (p. 10).

A feature of the MITTEN project called the Networked Learning Circle (NLC) parallels in small scale Goodlad's center of pedagogy idea. Project participants' work within one of five NLCs constitutes the core activity of the project. Additional events are designed to prepare participants for productive engagement within their respective NLCs and to provide venues for sharing the fruits of the NLC's collaborative efforts. This sequence of experiences is described in fuller detail, together with some rationale for these events.

Technology and Pedagogical Renewal: MITTEN's Conceptual Mooring

Remarkably, the typical student teaching or clinical experience has tended to foster–and at a most critical juncture in the pre-service teacher's preparation–distance rather than interaction between the pre-service teachers and their college and university-based faculty members. Certifying future teachers, having concluded all or nearly all of their course work, are "released" by their academic instructors into the hands of their hosting teachers. Also, regularly a supervising teacher who the student teacher's college or university appoints has an important role in supporting the pre-service teacher and, to varying degrees, in helping synthesize the student teacher's experiences with content and pedagogical knowledge already learned. Yet, like the student teachers themselves, these supervisors rarely have sustained contact during the clinical experience with members of the faculty mainstream. This structured separation has negative consequences of at least two sorts. First, the pre-service teacher is unable to benefit from meaningful continuing contact with content and pedagogical expertise. Second and perhaps even more limiting, the faculty members themselves are unable under most prevailing models to reconnect with the P-12 world in ways that might inform and rejuvenate their own instruction. Smith and Kaltenbaugh (1996) have noted the desirability of establishing the meaningful input of "academicians, master teachers, and master practitioners" to overcome the tendency for each of these vital participants in teacher education to stand as an "autonomous unit" (p. 96). Venues that can foster genuine dialogue between and among pre-service teachers and members of these three groups are necessary elements of programs aimed at spurring structural change. Goodlad's model provides a basis for pursuing this kind of cooperative engagement.

Thus, while the infusion of educational technology is MITTEN's end in view, the student teacher and the student teaching experience lie at the heart of MITTEN's plan for reaching this goal. Figure 2 (an adaptation of Figure 1 based on Goodlad) depicts the composition of MITTEN's NLCs and reflects the project's emphasis on the pre-service teacher's student teaching experience and his/her development of technology-enhanced lessons. The NLC idea calls for engaging four types of participants (as Figure 2 further illustrates): the student teachers themselves; practitioner experts comprised of the student teachers' school-based mentoring teacher and their university-based field supervisors; content area faculty of the arts and sciences, specializing in the student teachers' major fields of study; and education faculty specializing in educational technology and methods. This diversity of groups engaged in the focal activity of the grant seeks to enable the development of shared meaning, which Fullan (2001b) has identified as key in reaching outcomes related to educational change.

FIGURE 2. The "Networked Learning Circle": a structure for collaboration on technology integration, adapted from Goodlad (1994).

Content experts: arts and sciences faculty	Student teachers and their technology-enhanced lessons.	Methods and education technology experts: education faculty
	Practitioner experts: school-based master teachers; college-based student teaching supervisors	

The project's prevailing attention to the student teacher and the student teaching experience has certain strengths. Foremost among these, it helps MITTEN address the insularized nature of the student teaching experience. As mentioned, the clinical experience has most often tended to feature detachment between the postsecondary and the P-12 educational worlds rather than engagement, interaction, and collaboration on the pre-service teacher's behalf. A further important intention of this element of the design is that it leverages and reshapes existing relationships, practices, and energies rather than seeking to replace or to duplicate them. For example, the student teaching appointment has, as a state-mandated part of the certification experience, been a long-standing fixture of the college's teacher preparation programs. As such, the college has a well-seasoned field placement office. This office plays an important role in securing the interest and participation of student teachers, their hosting teachers, and their university-based supervisors.

Another prominent element of the project's design is that each of the NLCs stresses a distinct content area, corresponding to the instructional majors of the participating student teachers in each group. Accordingly, at the heart of the MITTEN project is a learning circle in each of the five following areas: early childhood/educational psychology, mathematics, social studies, language arts, and science. This cluster of five learning circles is depicted in Figure 3. A common criticism of teacher preparation programs that this element of the MITTEN model addresses is that often pedagogical concerns are detached from the world of subject area learning, undermining the adequate blending of the two to facilitate the development of what Shulman (1986) has described as pedagogical content knowledge. A further strength of this element of the project design is that it allows for some diversity of participants in terms of their instructional levels, since the focus is on the subject area rather than the grade level. The NLC experience therefore augments the more typical focus on grade level concerns, giving participating teachers early exposure to topics such as optimizing learning across age and grade levels, gaining insights into methods for accommodating diverse abilities among their P-12 students, and so forth.

Cycles of Progress: Project Events and Sequence

MITTEN's primary goal is to prepare a cadre of future educators with improved knowledge, skills, and confidence regarding the integration of information technology into the teaching and learning process in meaningful ways. MITTEN pursues its goal by offering three types of

FIGURE 3. MITTEN's five parallel "Networked Learning Circles," which provided for content-area focus.

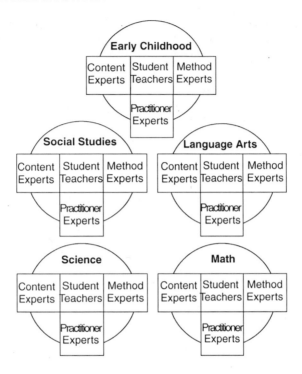

interrelated professional development activities to pre-service teachers, in-service teachers, and education faculty: a series of capacity-building workshops, a sequence of meetings of the NLCs themselves, and a pair of seminar activities designed for the whole-group engagement of all participants. Figure 4 shows the sequence of these events within a single cycle of the project. To stress again, the meetings of the NLCs and the work undertaken within them are of primary importance to the project. The other sorts of activities, however, constitute important supports to that work.

As is now true of the majority of the U.S. postsecondary teacher preparation programs (Vagale, 1995), UM-D certification students are required to have completed a core course in educational technology prior to their clinical phase. The MITTEN leadership is therefore familiar with the technological capacities of the student teachers who agree to participate in the project. In order to address the needs of the project's

FIGURE 4. One round of MITTEN events.

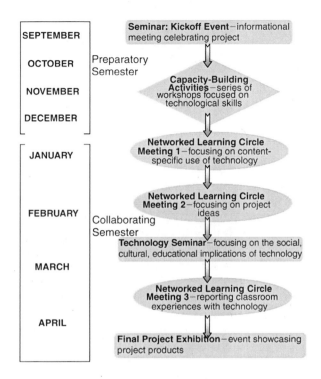

cooperating master teachers, field supervisors, methods and arts and sciences faculty members, however, MITTEN offers a set of capacity-building activities such as whole group workshops, working lunch sessions, and one-on-one mentoring designed to enhance the technology proficiency of these participants. The general scope of these sessions encompasses three needs areas–telecommunications tools, productivity tools, and educational multimedia–while specific emphases correspond to the needs that participants identify on needs assessments surveys. Thus, the capacity-building activities address technology-related professional development and training imperatives that various scholars (e.g., Willis & Mehlinger, 1996; Flaba, Strudler, & Bean, 1999; Strudler, 1993) have identified as crucial. Referring again to Figure 4, the capacity-building activities are part of a preparatory semester which is geared toward enhancing the productivity of the NLCs when they meet in the collaborating semester that follows.

In addition to the project's capacity-building events and to a set of whole group events that include seminar activities and exposition events, meetings of the five content-focused Networked Learning Circles during the course of the collaborating semester comprise perhaps the most vital set of activities within the MITTEN project. With each NLC focused on one of five areas of specialty (language arts, social studies, science, math, or early childhood), the memberships of each circle bear a common interest in improving instruction pertaining to a discrete content area. Each of the five circles meets at minimum three times during the course of the term in order to design, revise, and implement technology-enriched instruction for use in educational practices (e.g., course or unit redesign in P-12, syllabi revision at the university level). Two key assumptions form a basis for the interaction and exchange of ideas within the NLC. First is the notion that all members of the group are primarily present as learners. Thus, although each circle's profile includes educators at different "levels," all have a stake in developing their own familiarity with technology applications and uses and in doing so by observing other members' progress on their own experiments with and uses of instructional technology. Technology requires continuing openness to learning, even among those who are closest to technological innovation. The second assumption that exemplifies the conceptual mooring of a successful NLC is that co-learning supports the learning of all the members of the NLC. The critical eyes of other members of a circle help develop capacities in each member to self-monitor and to critique one's self with an eye on improvement.

The seminar activities serve two different but complementary purposes. First, they build awareness of broader social issues related to instructional technology, with attention to topics such as the digital divide, technologically enhanced participation in learning communities (Levin, 1996), and the effects of the technology revolution upon the formation and uses of knowledge (Scott, Cole, & Engel, 1992; see also Maddux, Johnson, & Willis, 2001, for additional descriptions of critical perspectives and of other value-laden implications of technology use). Special and emerging uses of technology in special learning contexts are other possibilities for seminar sessions revolving around issues such as uses of technology with certain age groups (e.g., Wetzel & McLean, 1997) or confronting challenges associated with special types of learners (e.g., Willetts, 1992). For the school-based master teachers in particular, these opportunities augment their home schools' efforts to contribute to teachers' continuous learning (Darling-Hammond, 1998). A second purpose of seminar activities is to build and maintain the investment and commitment of those involved by showcasing current products and works in progress, consistent with Fullan's (2001a) observation that knowledge exchange is both a motivator and an integral attribute of the competent professional.

To integrate all the elements of the MITTEN activities, each participant creates an electronic portfolio documenting the development and implementation of technology-enhanced lessons and projects (leading to course or unit redesign in P-12 and syllabi revision at the university level) to demonstrate the extent and quality of personal growth.

THE MITTEN EXPERIENCE

The following sections of this paper describe the project participants, the data collection and analysis, and findings from the first three cohort groups who were involved in the study from September 1, 2001, to April 30, 2003.

During the project's first three cohorts, 50 UM-D student teachers participated in the study, 18 in the first group, 15 in the second group, and 17 in the third group. Each student teacher participant was a member of one of five NLCs. All first-, second-, and third-round participants completed MITTEN expectations (coursework; capacity-building workshops; at least three circle meetings; required activities including implementation of technology-rich lessons, maintaining journals, and developing electronic portfolios; whole group activities including a kickoff event, a technology seminar focusing on a featured social issue, and a final exhibition showcasing project products).

Each student teacher's P-12 mentor teacher (called cooperating teachers) was a NLC participant. Eighteen (18) in round one, 15 in round two, and 17 in round three participated in the study. Cooperating teachers were partners in the project with the student teachers. They participated in all seminar, capacity-building, and NLC activities; they reflected on learning in journals and demonstrated achievements in integrating technology into lessons and projects through their electronic portfolios.

Each NLC consisted of one educational technology faculty, one methods faculty, one or two content faculty, and one student teaching supervisor from the participating schools and colleges. The MITTEN program targeted 18 university-level faculty and 5 student teaching supervisors to participate for a full year cycle (four semesters in two different cohort groups) in the project, while the student teachers and their mentors were involved for two semesters in one cohort group. This was perhaps to provide more experiences to higher education faculty. Fifteen (15) faculty started in the first year, with 13 finishing. Five (5) supervisors started in the first year, with four (4) completing the project. These faculty and field supervisors have been full participants in seminars, capacity-building activities, the NLC activities, journaling, and preparing the electronic portfolios that demonstrate the development and implementation of advanced technology lessons and projects in their teaching. Thirteen (13) new faculty and four (4) new supervisors started in the second-year cycle.

The qualitative data that contribute to the interpretive findings reported here came from a variety of sources. These include journal entries, technology projects, and reflections within electronic portfolios. Data collection and analysis were conducted on a continuous basis throughout the study. The cycle, that is, began with data collection, continued through reflection and analysis, and then looped back through additional data collection. The number of data sources and the frequency of the data collection effort helped to triangulate the data. The project objectives drove the data collection and analysis.

Findings suggest that the professional development activities taken place within the MITTEN program have been effective. Capacity-building activities increased participants' confidence and competence with technology tools. NLCs provided critical support for teaching with technology. Each of the NLCs fostered the development of technology-enhanced lessons while retaining both a content-specific mooring and pedagogical integrity. Within the NLCs, participant growth was evident in the exchange of ideas, increased communication and connection, and the emergence of a notable sense of community. Participants were engaged in seminar topics and these events successfully built awareness of pressing social issues. The following narrative illustrates the major findings in detail.

Technology-Proficient New Teachers

A major component of the MITTEN program was to prepare a new generation of P-12 teachers who are able to creatively and critically use technology to enhance student learning. Data suggest that MITTEN has definitely been a rewarding experience for pre-service teachers. The project provided the experiences needed for pre-service teachers to use advanced technology tools in their future practice.

Participants have fulfilled MITTEN expectations; namely, coursework, capacity-building workshops, and three circle meetings. Participants engaged in all required activities including implementation of technology-rich lessons, maintaining journals, and developing electronic portfolios. They also participated in seminar activities, including a kickoff event, a technology seminar focusing on digital divide (cohort #1), assistive technology (cohort #2), or on plagiarism and copyright issues in the digital age (cohort #3), and a final exhibition showcasing project products.

All pre-service teachers were required to take an educational technology course prior to the MITTEN program. Therefore, most student teachers were confident and competent with advanced technology tools. However, the needs assessment survey administered to them at the beginning of the MITTEN program revealed that most of the participating student teachers were at low to moderate skill levels in using advanced technology tools in the classroom. One student teacher put it best, "It is one thing to learn and use a program or tool, but it's another thing to teach it to a room full of six year olds."

Most student teachers took advantage of capacity-building workshops, even though they met the prerequisite for participation in the MITTEN project in their pre-service educational technology course. This was a good opportunity for them to remember what they learned in their educational technology course and/or to learn to use some advanced technology tools that were not introduced to them in such courses.

Observations in NLC discussions and the analysis of the journal entries indicated that NLCs provided critical support for teaching with technology. Within NLCs each student teacher planned and implemented an instructional unit consisting of at least five technology-integrated lessons. The NLCs provided student teachers with forums to present their units and receive feedback from the circle members. One student teacher's comments illustrate this point:

> My first impression of the group is that we are all open to sharing what we know about the project and any ideas. I feel like a team in this, which is much easier than doing it alone. . . . The ratio of faculty to students in our circle greatly benefits me. I am aware of the support given to me by the teachers, and plan to take advantage of their thoughts and ideas throughout this project.

There were wide disparities in both equipment and technical support among the participating schools districts. Student teachers collaborat-

ing with their classroom mentor teachers conducted site assessments using School Technology & Readiness (STaR) Charts (The CEO Forum
on Education and Technology, 2003), then developed their projects and
lessons to fit the limited resources at their disposal. The NLCs and the
National Educational Technology Standards for Students (International
Society for Technology in Education, 2000) within the limitations of
their teaching environments.

Most student teachers indicated that the MITTEN program demonstrated the importance of the technology integration in the classroom
and provided them the confidence and the competence to continue using
technology in their future classrooms. One student teacher explained:

> The MITTEN project has demonstrated the importance of inte-
> grating technology into the classroom. I have learned a great
> amount about technology and the various educational software
> programs there are for students. I feel that technology helps stu-
> dents to become better learners and provides a more effective way
> of teaching. Using technology for our unit has given the students
> the motivation to learn and the feeling of accomplishment for their
> work. I am very proud of the work they have completed and in the
> future I will continue to use technology in my own classroom.

Another student teacher expressed similar feelings:

> I am very happy that I decided to participate in the MITTEN proj-
> ect during student teaching. This experience will help me feel
> comfortable using technology in my future classroom. I have
> learned how to successfully create and integrate technology-based
> lessons into any existing curriculum. I feel that by participating in
> this project I have become a technology-proficient educator.

MITTEN therefore seems to meet a real need for student teachers to
become confident and competent enough to use advanced technology
tools in their future classrooms.

Technology-Proficient Practicing Teachers

Another major component of the MITTEN program was to increase
in-service teachers' ability to integrate information technology into their
curriculum and to mentor student teachers in using technology in a technology-rich environment. All P-12 mentor teachers were partners in the

project with their student teachers. Data suggest that MITTEN has been a significant staff development initiative for classroom mentor teachers.

All mentor teachers responded to a needs assessment survey that identified their needs and readiness to use technology in the classroom. Based on the data appropriate capacity-building activities were developed and conducted. Formal and informal interviews with classroom mentor teachers and analysis of journal entries revealed that capacity-building activities increased their confidence and competence with technology tools. The flexible format of the activities (group workshops, small-group work sessions, and one-on-one mentoring) helped to address individual needs. A number of cooperating teachers were assisted in Web search strategies, multimedia creativity programs, and visual thinking tools. One cooperating teacher expressed the feeling of many others as she reflected on her experience in capacity-building activities:

> I feel very comfortable learning this software in a step-by-step way. As I was in the session I noticed so many similarities between creating things in HyperStudio and working in PhotoAdobe and KidPix. I was confident in what I was doing because pieces of the program were familiar to me. I am finding that as I use these tools I am more confident in my abilities. Earlier this week I was able to send a photo, taken at school, to a parent through an attachment on e-mail. It was very exciting!

As was the intent of the capacity-building activities, participant growth was fairly common for those attending the sessions.

Observations in NLC discussions and analysis of journal entries revealed that NLCs provided critical support for classroom mentor teachers to learn about integrating technology into their classroom practice. The NLC discussions have made it abundantly clear that cooperating classroom teachers needed to look at models, and talk to those who used technology in their teaching. The following statement from one cooperating teacher illustrates this point:

> I enjoyed discussing the project ideas with our circle. One of the real benefits of this project is the opportunity to share ideas with the other teachers and professors.

Another cooperating teacher shared similar feelings:

> [My student teacher] and I worked out the details of our first three projects, and decided upon our final two before the meeting. We may even try to incorporate a few extra if there is time. I sincerely appreciate the spirit of collegiality we have as a group. Suggestions were offered about how we might better enhance our projects, and we plan on making some modifications. Teaching can be an isolating profession if you allow it. You see your colleagues during hall duty and for 20 minutes at lunch if you're lucky. This certainly doesn't allow time to share knowledge and exchange ideas. This NLC was worth my time.

These reflections indicate that NLCs were meeting a real need for cooperating classroom teachers to discuss their challenges and successes in a sustained fashion.

Most UM-D student teachers were more advanced in integrating technology than were their cooperating classroom teachers; consequently, the student teachers served in mentoring roles themselves with regard to using instructional technology. In return, cooperating school teachers assisted student teachers in accessing technology tools and (in some cases) the expertise of building technologists; they have helped student teachers link content standards with technology standards in carrying out projects and lessons with advanced teaching and learning techniques. One cooperating teacher's comment illustrates the feelings of many others:

> I am enthusiastic about learning more and that is why this project appeals to me! It's designed to assist veteran teachers by educating them about technology in a supportive environment. I have the classroom expertise as a master teacher while my student teacher has more experience using computers. We will absolutely learn from each other!

As it was the case for student teachers, the MITTEN program provided the experiences needed for classroom mentor teachers to learn about the effective use of advanced technology tools in the classroom.

Technology-Proficient Faculty

The MITTEN program was also aimed at increasing current teacher educators' ability to use technology to better prepare tomorrow's teachers and to model meaningful uses of technology in their professional practice. Data suggest that, at the beginning of the MITTEN program, most faculty were at low to moderate skill levels in using technology with students to meet their course objectives, as well as in using advanced technologies to enhance their personal and professional productivity. Their participation in capacity-building workshops, the NLC activities, and technology seminars increased the development and implementation of advanced technology lessons and projects in their teaching. Faculty electronic portfolios demonstrated that most participating faculty increased their instructional use of technology. This includes using Web pages, listserves, and discussion boards as a means of communicating with students; using software application tools in their classroom activities; and developing technology-related assessment tools. For example, an early childhood methods professor assigned her students to create children's portfolios using PowerPoint. This type of assessment is a crucial component to all early childhood programs. The portfolio is a record of the child's process of learning: what the child has learned and how s/he has gone about learning; how s/he thinks, questions, analyzes, synthesizes, produces, creates; and how s/he interacts intellectually, emotionally, and socially with others. The portfolios contain pictures, children's work samples, descriptions, children's voices, and an evaluation of the child. Students had to apply many technology skills to create such portfolios. The professor reflected on her experience in this project:

> I was so excited to figure out the Power Point program can be used to create children's developmental portfolios. The students [pre-service teachers] produced high quality developmental portfolios while using this tool. The electronic developmental portfolios can easily be shared with the parents in the classroom. Also each child's developmental portfolio can be archived and shared with future students. It makes perfect sense that technology integration activities must be connected to course content and assignments.

Some faculty who supervise student teachers have increased their instructional use of technology such as e-mail, listserves, and discussion boards as communication devices with student teachers and have become familiar with tools available to and used by P-12 teachers. One supervisor of student teachers described her experience:

Prior to participation in the MITTEN project, my computer technology skills consisted basically of use of MS Word for simple word-processing and a bit of e-mailing. During the past year, my skill proficiency has increased considerably as I now make use of many more Word capabilities, do Internet research, communicate and send files via e-mail, and use an online discussion board. In addition, my understanding and awareness of computer capabilities have increased enormously, so that I will continue to learn and use more in the future.

Despite their increased use of technology in their daily practice, some faculty have needed considerable time and professional development for moving beyond their traditional practice. One faculty member noted:

My participation has been a rich, rewarding experience, since I have greatly increased my knowledge of the technology issues in education and am currently implementing my enhanced skills in my upcoming courses, but I do have miles to go, as a famous poet once said.

It was evident from the faculty reflections and from the project exhibited on their electronic portfolios that most faculty appreciated the opportunities provided through MITTEN to master the tools to enhance their professional practice.

Technology Learning Resources

In addition to the preparation of technology-proficient P-16 educators, MITTEN also focused on developing a series of technology learning resources (including software tools, Web-based curriculum materials, hypermedia, and digital video best practice cases) that model effective uses of information technology for future teachers, practicing teachers, and teacher educators. Data suggest that most MITTEN participants developed and implemented exemplary technology-integrated projects (leading to course or unit redesign in P-12 and syllabi revision at the university level) and included them in their electronic portfolios. Projects created by the pre-service teachers and in-service teachers include reflections related to their development and effectiveness and directly related to National Educational Technology Standards for Students (NETS-S) and the state's curriculum standards. Portfolios from faculty members containing models for technology applications in university classrooms are also now available. The MITTEN Web page contains increasing numbers of such learning resources (http://www.umd.umich.edu/mitten).

Production of portfolios and lessons was certainly an anticipated outcome. Less anticipated, however, was the level of enthusiasm with which participants shared these technology resources. As one of many examples, a multi-age classroom teacher produced a "techno-book" (a PowerPoint slideshow exported to VHS format to be sent home) project with her students which inspired an early childhood teacher in a later cohort to create a similar project. More importantly, project participants have found more ways to share technology-learning resources including lesson plans and project ideas/examples at their P-16 buildings and with parents and the community. One example is that five MITTEN teams in different schools have presented their projects to the school community (inviting district administration and parents).

P-16 Partnerships

MITTEN envisioned forming a self-sustaining professional development network among future teachers, practicing teachers, and teacher educators to reach and use technology resources for further professional development. Data suggest that the communication and connections among project participants created a strong sense of community in most cases. Most project participants felt they had been working toward similar goals and had creative, supportive folks as partners on a common journey. They developed a shared vision about the use of technology for instruction.

In reviewing the structure of the teacher preparation experiences in place at UM-D prior to MITTEN, the project leadership discovered that, like most other institutions, many of the unit's practices and structures fostered distance rather than interaction between and among pre-service teachers, college and university-based faculty members including student teaching supervisors, and P-12 cooperating teachers. For example, student teachers' university-appointed "field supervisors" typically have little meaningful contact with full-time university faculty members. In short, structured separation of this sort has contributed to conditions in which a pre-service teacher and a P-12 cooperating teacher were unable to benefit from continuing contact with content and pedagogical experts at the university. In turn–and even more unsatisfactory–such structures of separation have prevented college and university faculty members from connecting with the P-12 world in ways that might inform and rejuvenate their own instruction. None of the several parties involved in teacher preparation–whether at the college/university level or in P-12 classrooms–have been receiving sustained and meaningful support of the sort that might adequately address the development and implementation of technology-rich lessons and projects. And, importantly, the status quo at UM-D prior to MITTEN reflected patterns of structured separation that are typical of teacher preparation programs across the country.

Formal and informal interviews with project participants and their journal entries indicated that the MITTEN model addressed these shortcomings by providing a venue that fostered genuine dialogue among participating faculty, P-12 teachers, student teachers, and their university supervisors. In so doing, the program was overcoming the tendency for each of these vital participants in teacher education to stand as an autonomous unit. Engaging these diverse groups through NLCs enabled the development of shared meaning, important in reaching outcomes related to pedagogical renewal in technology education. One student teaching supervisor reflected on her experience:

> 3rd NLC Meeting. This is a wonderful group of people to work with. There is such good rapport and interaction among the members. . . . It's marvelous to see all these educators sharing ideas and inspiring each other. It is revitalizing all our teaching.

One cooperating teacher similarly expressed her feelings:

> I enjoyed discussing the project ideas with our circle. One of the real benefits of this project is the opportunity to share ideas with the other teachers and professors.

These reflections indicate that NLCs were meeting a real need for teachers to communicate and collaborate with their P-16 colleagues.

Numerous examples of communication and collaboration were observed of university faculty who had little such connection prior to MITTEN–even though these people have discovered that they often have the same goals and in many cases the same students. An example: a science-methods faculty member volunteered to visit the P-12 science team to provide assistance in their classroom. Yet another: Three faculty from Henry Ford Community College reported a "significant increase" in their collaboration because of MITTEN. The project provided opportunities to address a concern, expressed in one journal entry, that "university and college faculty do not know what is happening in public schools; they are living in their own, isolated worlds." Similarly P-12 teachers and pre-service teachers had opportunities to learn and appreciate the resources and perspectives the teacher educators brought to teaching and learning.

University faculty have expressed appreciation of the opportunity MITTEN affords them to collaborate and communicate with each other and to connect with P-12 teachers and student teachers in ways which inform and rejuvenate their own instruction.

MITTEN IN PERSPECTIVE

The question currently challenging the teacher education community is not whether technology should be included in teacher preparation, but what is the efficient way to integrate technology into the teacher education curriculum. Starting in 1999, the U.S. Department of Education's PT3 initiative provided the educational technology community with the opportunity to explore and develop a variety of approaches for addressing technology integration into teacher preparation. The MITTEN model presented and discussed in this paper represents a strong theoretical grounding as a response to the PT3 call, highlighting the three critical components of technology integration into the teacher preparation programs—core course work, effective faculty modeling of instructional technology, and technology-enriched field experiences. John Goodlad's discussion about "center of pedagogy" has provided a basis for pursuing the MITTEN model that fosters a structure for collaboration on technology integration. The work of the student teachers and student teaching lie at the heart of the NLC. The NLC model facilitates engagement, interaction, and collaboration among schools of education, school districts, and colleges of arts and sciences, on the pre-service teachers' behalf, and it undoes the kind of detachment between the postsecondary and the K-12 educational worlds. This type of cooperative engagement among all of these entities warrants addressing all three critical elements of technology integration into a teacher preparation program.

Findings from the first three cohorts of the project indicate that the MITTEN model provides a venue that fosters genuine dialogue among academicians, P-12 teachers, and student teachers and their university supervisors. Engaging these diverse groups through NLCs enables the development of shared meaning, important in reaching outcomes related to pedagogical renewal in technology education. In these ways, the MITTEN model enables an effective response to the need for a more comprehensive program for the preparation of a technology-proficient P-16 teaching force. Indicators of the MITTEN model's effectiveness in enhancing technology proficiency include observed increases in the quality of participants' portfolios. Further, the project has brought significant growth in the numbers of portfolios both submitted and accepted for formal state recognition. Capacity-building activities, meanwhile, have increased the participants' confidence and competence with advanced technology tools. And, technology seminars built awareness of pressing social issues. The communication and connections among project participants has created a strong sense of community. The research reported here suggests that, in these ways, the present model enables an effective response to the need for a more comprehensive program for the preparation of a technology-proficient P-16 teaching force.

REFERENCES

Darling-Hammond, L. (1998). Teacher learning that supports student learning. *Educational Leadership, 55*(5), 6-11.

Duran, M. (2000). Examination of technology integration into an elementary teacher education program: One university's experience. (Doctoral dissertation, Ohio University, 2000). *Dissertation Abstracts International, A-61/07*, 2664.

Flaba, C. J., Strudler, N. B., Bean, T. W. (1999). Choreographing change one step at a time: Reflections on integrating technology into teacher education. *Action in Teacher Education, 21*(1), 61-76.

Fullan, M. (2001a). *Learning in a culture of change.* San Francisco: Jossey-Bass.

Fullan, M. (2001b). *The new meaning of educational change* (3rd ed.). New York: Teachers College Press.

Goodlad, J. I. (1994). *Educational renewal: Better teachers, better schools.* San Francisco: Jossey-Bass.

Gunn, C. (1991). Curriculum integration project: An evolving model. In D. Carey, R. Carey, D. Willis, & J. Willis (Eds.), *Technology and teacher education annual, 1991* (pp. 27-29). Charlottesville, VA: Association for the Advancement of Computing in Education.

Holmes Group. (1995). *Tomorrow's schools of education.* East Lansing, MI: Author.

Hunt, N. (1994). Intention and implications: The impact of technology coursework in elementary classroom. In J. Willis, B. Robin, & D. Willis (Eds.), *Technology and teacher education annual, 1994* (pp. 38-41). Charlottesville, VA: Association for the Advancement of Computing in Education.

International Society for Technology in Education (ISTE). (2000). *National educational technology standards for students: Connecting curriculum and technology.* Eugene, OR: ISTE Publications.

Instructional Technology Resource Center. (1998, January). *Integration of technology in pre-service teacher education programs: The southern and island regional profile.* Orlando, FL: College of Education, University of Central Florida.

Kim, C. S., & Peterson, D. (1992). The introductory computer course: Business majors perceived importance of topics. *Journal of Education for Business, 6*(6), 361-365.

Levin, H. M. (1996). Accelerated schools: The background. In C. Finnan, E. P. St. John, J. McCarthy, & S. P. Slovacek (Eds.), *Accelerated schools in action: Lessons from the field* (pp. 3-23), Thousand Oaks, CA: Corwin Press.

Maddux, C. D., Johnson, D. L., & Willis, J. W. (2001). *Educational computing: Learning with tomorrow's technologies* (3rd ed.). Boston: Allyn & Bacon.

Moursund, D. G., & Bielefeldt, T. (1999). *Will new teachers be prepared to teach in a digital age? A national survey on information technology in teacher education.* Eugene, OR: International Society for Technology in Education.

National Council for Accreditation of Teacher Education. (1997). *Technology and the new professional teacher: 21st century classroom.* Retrieved September 22, 2005, from http://www.ncate.org/public/technology21.asp?ch=113.

Novak, D., & Berger, C. F. (1991). Integrating technology into teacher education. *T. H. E. Journal, 18*(9), 83-86.

O'Bannon, B., Matthew, K. I., & Thomas, L. (1998). Faculty development: Key to the integration of technology in teacher education. *Journal of Computing in Teacher Education, 14*(4), 7-11.

Scott, T., Cole, M., & Engle, M. (1992). Computers and education: A cultural constructivist perspective. In G. Grant (Ed.), *Review of Research in Education, 18,* 191-251.

Shulman, L. S. (1986). Paradigms and research programs in the study of teaching. In M. C. Wittrock (Ed.), *Handbook of research on teaching* (3rd ed., pp. 3-36). New York: MacMillan.

Smith, D. B., & Kaltenbaugh, L. P. S. (1996). University-school partnership: Reforming teacher preparation. In J. P. Comer, N. M. Haynes, E. T. Joyner, & M. Ben-Avie (Eds.), *Rallying the whole village: The Comer process for reforming education* (pp. 72-97). New York: Teachers College Press.

Strudler, N. (1993). Staff development and technology: A position paper. *Journal of Computing in Teacher Education, 9*(4), 8-10.

Strudler, N., & Wetzel, K. (1999). Lessons from exemplary colleges of education: Factors affecting technology integration in pre-service programs. *Educational Technology Research and Development, 74*(4), 63-81.

The CEO Forum on Education and Technology. (2003). *School technology & readiness (STaR) charts.* Retrieved September 22, 2005, from http://www.iste.org/starchart

Vagle, R. (1995). Technology instruction for pre-service teachers: An examination of exemplary programs. In D. A. Willis, B. Robin, & J. Willis (Eds.), *Technology and teacher education annual, 1995* (pp. 230-237). Charlottesville, VA: Association for the Advancement of Computing in Education.

Wepner, S. B., & Mobley, M. M. (1998). Reaping new harvests: Collaboration and communication through field experiences. *Action in Teacher Education, 20*(3), 50-61.

Wetzel, K. (1993). Teacher educators' uses of computers in teaching. *Journal of Technology and Teacher Education, 1*(4), 335-352.

Wetzel, K., & McLean, S. (1997). Early childhood teacher preparation: A tale of authors and multimedia, a model of technology integration described. *Journal of Computing in Childhood Education, 8*(1), 39-58.

Wilburg, K. M. (1997). The dance of change: Integrating technology in classrooms. *Computers in the Schools, 13*(1-2), 171-184.

Willetts, K. (1992). *Technology and second language learning* (Report No. EDO FL 92-07). Washington, DC: Office of Educational Research and Improvement. (ERIC Document Reproduction Service No. ED 350883)

Willis, J. W., & Mehlinger, H. D. (1996). Information technology and teacher education. In J. Sickle, T. J. Buttery, & E. Guyton (Eds.), *Handbook of research on teacher education* (pp. 978-1029). New York: Macmillan.

doi:10.1300/J025v23n03_03

Bruce Havelock
David Gibson
Lorraine Sherry

The Personal Learning Planner: Collaboration Through Online Learning and Publication

SUMMARY. This paper discusses the online Personal Learning Planner (PLP) project underway at the National Institute of Community Innovations (NICI), one of the partners in the Teacher Education Network (TEN), a 2000 PT3 Catalyst grantee. The Web-based PLP provides a standards-linked "portfolio space" for both works in progress and demonstration collections of completed work, combined with structures to support mentorship and advising centered around the improvement of work. In this paper, we describe the PLP's history and rationale, design, and some initial results of its use in pilot programs, discussing the implications of lessons learned through these pilot experiences that can inform the PLP's effective use in teacher education. Early lessons from the field show the cultural, pedagogical, and technological challenges and

---

BRUCE HAVELOCK is Research Associate, RMC Research Corporation, Denver, CO 80202 (E-mail: havelock@rmcdenver.com).
DAVID GIBSON is Founder & President, CurveShift, Stowe, VT 05672 (E-mail: david.gibson@curveshift.com).
LORRAINE SHERRY is Senior Research Associate, RMC Research Corporation, Denver, CO 80202 (E-mail: sherry@rmcdenver.com).

[Haworth co-indexing entry note]: "The Personal Learning Planner: Collaboration Through Online Learning and Publication." Havelock, Bruce, David Gibson, and Lorraine Sherry. Co-published simultaneously in *Computers in the Schools* (The Haworth Press, Inc.) Vol. 23, No. 3/4, 2006, pp. 55-70; and: *Teaching Teachers to Use Technology* (ed: D. LaMont Johnson, and Kulwadee Kongrith) The Haworth Press, Inc., 2006, pp. 55-70. Single or multiple copies of this article are available for a fee from The Haworth Document Delivery Service [1-800-HAWORTH, 9:00 a.m. - 5:00 p.m. (EST). E-mail address: docdelivery@haworthpress.com].

potentials of basing performance reviews on collaboratively generated, standards-linked, Web-based portfolio processes, and products.
doi:10.1300/J025v23n03_04 *[Article copies available for a fee from The
Haworth Document Delivery Service: 1-800-HAWORTH. E-mail address:
<docdelivery@haworthpress.com> Website: <http://www.HaworthPress.com>
© 2006 by The Haworth Press, Inc. All rights reserved.]*

KEYWORDS. Electronic portfolio, performance assessment, personalization, mentorship, cognitive apprenticeship, teacher education

The Personal and Professional Learning Planner and Portfolio (PLP),
with support from the National Institute for Community Innovations
(NICI), has been available since 2002 and piloted in pre-service teacher
education programs, K-12 schools, regional service centers, and other
local educational agencies. This tool for collaboratively discussing and
improving student work, linking that work to goals and standards, and
collecting it in a Web-based portfolio format is uniquely suited to some
of the challenges surrounding authentic assessment, digital literacy, and
collaborative reflection in teacher education. In this paper, we discuss
the utility of the PLP in teacher education; the PLP's theoretical framework, design history, and goals; and some early results of its implementation in a variety of institutional contexts. Lessons from these varied
contexts serve to illuminate challenges and future goals that will augment the PLP's effectiveness in supporting a continuum of teacher
learning from pre-service coursework through the duration of the
teaching career.

ELECTRONIC PORTFOLIOS
TO SUPPORT TEACHER LEARNING

The need for a Web-based tool focused on the improvement of
pre-service teacher work has two parts. First, learners benefit from feedback that comes from a diverse audience, yet pre-service and induction
programs often have limited resources and structures that result in scant
feedback to aspiring teachers. In these cases, the work of aspiring teachers frequently evolves in relative isolation, potentially solidifying patterns of work that do not naturally include constructive feedback as a
natural part of work, leading to the oft-lamented isolated teaching con-

dition that persists in many schools today. A Web-based professional network can both help overcome this isolation, and, just as importantly, it can provide the future teacher with high-quality information that might otherwise be unavailable. The feedback from multiple perspectives thus enabled can help teachers reflect on multiple dimensions of their work.

Secondly, our goals for pre-service teacher education are evolving toward sophisticated understandings of demanding and complex material. In addition to mastering subject matter, thorough teacher education requires the development of a critical and reflective stance toward the work of teaching and toward one's own progress therein. To support this important work, assessment of pre-service and ongoing teacher education must evolve to match. In small, personalized teacher preparation programs, pre-service teachers may benefit from interviews, observation, and feedback sessions related to their work; but in many programs that experience is limited to the last few months of preparation. Too often, assessment of pre-service teacher learning is a one-way interaction that takes place at a single point in time–usually the end of a course in the pre-service curriculum. Ideally, assessment should play a meaningful part in the ongoing learning of the person being assessed, while providing information that helps advisors and mentors to support the learner's education. Rather than an isolated measurement of skills or knowledge, effective assessment should be dynamic and ongoing, forming an integral part of the learning process (Shepard, 2000). This kind of effective and authentic educational assessment should record problems encountered, decisions considered and made, and the validation of the work produced–not just the final outcome.

The dynamic online collaboration supported by the PLP performs these functions while also putting the learner in a position of control of and responsibility for a dialogue with advisors around his or her own learning. The PLP aims to create a longitudinal multimedia record of growth and change in an aspiring teacher's skills and capabilities. As such, the PLP can potentially document a future teacher's progress through the learning/adoption trajectory (Sherry, Billig, Tavalin, & Gibson, 2000), from learner to adopter, co-learner, reaffirmer, and leader.

Although not widespread, portfolios have been embraced in some corners of pre-service teacher education (cf. Andrews, Ducharme, & Cox, 2002). Among the purposes relevant to teacher education that electronic portfolios can serve are Barrett's (1998) diagnosis of student learning, grading or proficiency testing, promotion or certification, or as an aid to the job-seeking process. Yet while the American Association of Higher Education in 2003 reported that 61 institutions of higher education use electronic portfolios in some form, few if any institutions integrate all of the functions of meaningful reflection, ongoing dialogue, and a platform for both ongoing and completed products.

The PLP provides a "portfolio space" for works in progress and demonstration collections of work, and multiple channels for communicating around their creation, revision, and assessment. By flexibly serving these functions, the PLP is robust enough to meet the demands of ongoing, dynamic, authentic assessment of growth in teacher knowledge and skills. The online PLP allows all media formats, and a multiplicity of linkages among learning goals or standards of performance, projects, and the evidence of attainment of those goals and standards. Distinct from electronic portfolios that concentrate on the presentation and storage of completed work, the PLP concentrates on the continuous improvement of work and the documentation of that improvement over time.

PROJECT HISTORY

The Web-based application at the heart of the PLP was developed by Gibson with funding from the Preparing Tomorrow's Teachers to Use Technology (PT3) program, as well as from work funded by the National Science Foundation, private funding and the Technology Innovation Challenge Grant program. The lineage of the PLP comes from two sources. One source was a bold move by a local secondary school community in Montpelier, Vermont, which in 1993 placed "individualized educational plans for every student" into its long-term strategic plan. In 1995, this led to the creation and implementation of a school-wide program to place personal learning at the center of a continuous conversation involving all students, their parents or guardians, and caring adults in a school. The University of Vermont provided support and energy to this school-based development through the writings of researchers and theorists such as Bentley (1999), Moffat (1998), Friedrichs (2000), and Gibson (1999, 2000).

In addition, early in its development, the concept of the Montpelier "PLP" was picked up by the Regional Laboratory at Brown University and combined with similar movements and interests in Rhode Island, Maine, Massachusetts, and other New England states. In Maine, for example, the concept of personal learning took on a primary role in that state's new proposal for the reform of secondary schools. In other work of the Regional Laboratory, the theme of personalization became a crucial feature of the secondary school reform network in the region, and was tied to the principles of *Breaking Ranks*, the reform monograph of the National Association of Secondary School Principals. Thus, the concept of personalization of learning as essential to educational reform is well founded in theory as well as in practice.

The PLP's second thread of lineage came from the pioneering work of the WEB Project, which used Web-based tools and networked communities to share and critique original student work online. The WEB Project provided a rich research base with which to explore online dialogue and design conversations within a virtual community of learners and to define the path by which teachers progress from learners to leaders with technology (Sherry, 2000; Sherry, Tavalin, & Billig, 2000; Sherry et al., 2000). The WEB Project established a system that linked 10 participating schools and districts (including Montpelier High School) and multiple cooperating initiatives in online discussions of student work. Art and music students posted works in progress and received constructive feedback from community practitioners and learners, based on their articulated intentions for their works-in-progress. Middle school students from three schools across Vermont conducted book discussions, facilitated by staff from the Vermont Center for the Book and their teachers. Teachers discussed challenges, conducted action research, shared results, and co-developed rubrics to assess instructional processes, progress, and outcomes. Through these efforts, the WEB Project contributed substantially to knowledge of effective practice for conducting online dialogue and design conversations.

Through the WEB Project, teachers developed connections with and drew on the expertise of other practitioners in their discipline from participating initiatives throughout the state. For example, art teachers and students shared online interactions with traditional artists, graphic artists, and multimedia designers; and music teachers and students carried on conversations with resident musicians, music teachers, and composers. The mentor-practitioners, in turn, were asked to give students feedback and essentially became co-instructors in the course. This learning community resembled an apprenticeship model, but it allowed for many mentors and was not constrained by time or place.

The secrets of the WEB Project's success were many, but it is worth highlighting the singular focus on creation of original student work, which ensured that online dialogue remained centered around the learner (Sherry, 2000; Sherry et al., 2000). In the WEB Project, "student work" included two important genres:

- *student-created works* of traditional art, digital art, multimedia, and music, supported by *student-initiated design conversations* with teachers, peers, and experts; and
- *student-moderated dialogue* with reflective, threaded discussions about assigned language arts texts that focused on controversial issues faced by middle school students.

In the design conversations, the entire sequence of activity only began if and when a student shared a work-in-progress and asked for specific feedback. If the work was shared too early, the request for feedback and the ensuing online interactions with experts was too general and superficial. On the other hand, if the request for feedback came too late, when the work was already in its final form, the conversation was viewed by the learner as unimportant or too critical. However, if the student requested feedback at some optimum point when the work was already posted on the WEB Project's Web site in draft form, and if he or she was able to articulate specific design problems that needed prompt attention, the community of experts was able to provide a useful range of practical suggestions to be filtered, evaluated, and used for revision and refinement of the work-in-progress. These qualities of learner-centeredness, creativity, self-initiative, and intellectual focus were carried forward by Gibson into the PLP.

THE PERSONAL LEARNING PORTFOLIO: DESIGN RATIONALE

The PLP is based on a theory of dialogue articulated by Gibson and Friedrichs (Friedrichs, 2000; Friedrichs & Gibson, 2001). Friedrichs (2000) discussed four distinct dialogue states for which supports were explicitly built into the PLP:

1. *Sharing experience*–listening to one's own and others' inner speech and natural attitude about a skill or concept;
2. *Expressing and examining diverse concepts*–recognizing conflicts; analyzing old and new concepts, models, and beliefs; working in one's zone of proximal development;

3. *Articulating applications and understandings*–practicing new skills; combining old and new concepts; using others' ideas; using scaffolds to renegotiate understandings; and
4. *Communicating new powers and creations*–celebrating effects of critical analysis.

The premise of collaborative interaction as a basis for learning is consistent with research focused on authenticity, use of technology to create problem-centered learning teams, representation of complex dynamics in educational settings, and e-learning (Carroll, 2000; Gibson, 1999; Gibson & Clarke, 2000; NSDC, 2001; Newmann & Wehlage, 1995; Sherry & Myers, 1998; Stiggins, 1997; Wiggins, 1989).

The learner's productivity and self-efficacy is the ultimate goal of the online PLP. Work samples are the critical source for evidence of learning, the documentation of progress, and the verification that high standards have been achieved. By placing student work at the center of the PLP, the learner is pushed to a higher standard of personal accountability for the publicly visible quality of that work.

In the PLP, learners pose questions to advisors; they develop, use, and compare the value of a variety of learning assets–their strengths, interests, aspirations, and community and personal resources–and they retain ultimate control over the progress of their work, the integration of feedback they receive, and its ultimate publication. This decision-making power enhances learner motivation and develops a sense of ownership of work products, resulting in final products of higher quality.

With these concepts of learning in mind, and with funding from the U.S. Department of Education under the PT3 program, NICI developed the first version of the PLP as a "critical friends" online space to help future teachers assemble portfolios of evidence showing that they meet the standards required for a teaching credential or license. The PLP is designed to assist aspiring teachers through the processes of:

- *self-assessing* strengths, interests, and aspirations and their relationship to program requirements;
- *planning* pre-service education learning goals and projects;
- *linking* goals and projects to valued outcome standards;
- *creating* original multimedia work samples and sharing those with others;
- *receiving* high-quality feedback from mentors, advisors, or other critical friends for the consideration of their learning goals, im-

provement of their work, and strengthening of their knowledge and skills;

- *documenting* and validating the achievement of learning goals; and
- *selecting* and preparing exhibits of learning.

The PLP includes tools for online survey building and administration, developing local standards and rubrics, organizing uploaded work in relation to those standards and rubrics, forming learners and advisors into various communities, and creating a completed Web-based portfolio product. The PLP can be flexibly customized to serve the needs of practically any outcome-oriented collaborative learning group. While most electronic portfolios demonstrate either formative or summative learning, the PLP showcases both.

In practice, learners in the PLP system articulate their goals for learning, reference those goals to standards for work or knowledge introduced into the PLP by program administrators, and upload computer files to the PLP server that exhibit their progress toward meeting these goals and standards. Through a process of collaborative reflection, assessment, and several iterations of multiple work products, learners develop an electronic portfolio showing their growth and abilities; this portfolio is then available to them as an exhibit of their growth and an aid to their future career progression.

"Advisors" and "Learners" exhibit specific technical characteristics in the context of the PLP. Through the management interface, Advisors are associated with one or more Learners. When a Learner's goal or work is being shared for critique and feedback, the Advisor can discuss, offer direct edits, or validate the goal or work as adequate for its purpose. For example, an Advisor might validate a goal as appropriate for completion of a secondary teaching license in science, and validate a piece of work as evidence of achieving a standard of performance linked to one or more goals. The validation process can be formalized with rubrics or entered as narrative. Any rubric can be linked with any piece of work as evidence. When a group of Advisors scores work using a common rubric, a summative rubric can then be built upon completion of their work.

EARLY EXPERIMENTS IN PLP USE

As the PLP evolves, so do its potential applications. While it is difficult to argue that any technology is entirely value-free, the flexibility of the PLP allows for its customization to fit the values of the groups that use it. In this section, we explore five such applications in very different contexts, aiming to draw from this range of experiences lessons that can inform the PLP's continuing design and enhancement to support pre-service teacher education.

In summer 2002, 31 sites were using the online PLP in support of an extensive range of educational programs and networks. Five of these sites were selected to explore initial reception of and reactions to the PLP. To explore the boundaries of the PLP's flexibility, the sites were selected to illustrate the issues involved with customizing the PLP to meet the distinct needs of five very different learning communities.

Fourteen participating program administrators completed surveys and were interviewed about their experience with the PLP. From the PLP environment itself, we examined (from six programs) the uploaded program standards, the list of rubrics for evaluating learner work, the surveys that had been created and administered within the PLP sites, and a number of individual learners' PLP pages that contained the work of individuals and the commentaries of their mentors or advisors. Initial analysis of these data led to the generation of several hypotheses about the critical trends in PLP implementation. The data were then re-examined to extract trends and potential lessons to guide the PLP's future development and implementation.

Initial results affirmed that the PLP can effectively meet the needs of a wide range of users. All five program administrators felt that the purpose and functions of the PLP were appropriate, useful, effective, powerful, and well suited to their intended audiences. After getting past the initial hurdles of training and basic system familiarity, users found that the PLP resonated with their ideas about cognitive coaching, peer mentoring, standards-based instruction, and social learning. Pilot users also found the design and management approach adopted by the PLP design team to be very effective. All five pilot users described a high level of support, responsiveness, and personal attention from the design team.

By the end of 2002, several more institutions had begun to use the PLP. At two of these sites, potentially richer data were generated than had been available for two of the initial five sites explored; the summaries below include two new sites and three that were already using the PLP by summer 2002. For each group of learners, distinctive features of the pilot experience (as described by program administrators and research staff) are summarized.

- *Eighth-grade students in a public middle school.* A primary goal in this program was to "boost student engagement. . . . By working through the goal setting and reflection process, [students] will be able to articulate what they want to get out of school." Supported by a dedicated program leader (who is also the technical administrator), students in this group seemed undaunted by the technical challenges, and posted more work than any other single group in this sample, often proceeding through several drafts. Comments from teachers, while initially somewhat superficial, began to show more substance as the process of providing online comments on student work became more familiar to them.
- *Attendees at an intensive two-day professional conference session.* The goal in this case was to extend professional learning that had been initiated at a regional conference; however, the PLP was also used here to prepare for a more effective conference-based learning experience. The session leader was able to review individual learning goals for nearly all of the session participants before the conference took place, and alter her instructional plan for the conference to accommodate those needs. After the conference, the attendees continued to serve as a community of learners, providing input and advice on one another's work and extending the learning afforded by the conference.
- *School administrators working with a regional service organization.* Though this group uploaded no work in their early stages of PLP use, they completed a large number of surveys. The program administrator attributed this to the fact that the surveys were analogous to an exit interview protocol that was part of the existing program. Similarly, this administrator focused on the "4-step work cycle" of the PLP because it nicely matched the "4-step learning cycle" that was an existing component of her program. The PLP was set up for teams of administrators to function together as "Learner" units. As these administrators in general communicated infrequently and were geographically dispersed, the PLP provided for "greater continuity between sessions and a sense of measurable progress."
- *Ph.D. students in an educational leadership program.* While no state standards existed for doctoral students in this field, students developed their own goals and standards for graduation (four mandatory areas and three areas chosen by students) with input from their advisory committees, and made early steps toward organizing their works around those goals through the PLP. Students in

this program requested to be able to give each other feedback, so all were given system rights as both Learners and Advisors. Some students started the process by giving each other "fake" feedback to test the system, but comments tended to develop more substance over time. Learners also started to personalize their PLP portal pages and requested more flexibility in doing so. Participants in the program felt that the program as a whole had an attitude that encouraged getting feedback for revision, which increased receptivity to the PLP.

- *Pre-service teachers in a preparation program for urban teachers.* In this program, candidates posted their inquiries and their action research projects while building a profile that was provided to hiring school systems as evidence of their competence. While initially, prospective teachers in this program were not overtly enthusiastic about improving works in progress for portfolio inclusion, the program administrator exerted considerable effort to make it clear that learners' PLP work could play a crucial role in getting a job, and that school systems were very interested in seeing documentation of learner growth. It became clear in the job market that participants who did develop portfolios through the PLP had a distinct advantage over those who did not. The administrator then began lobbying locally to have official program credit awarded for PLP portfolio development, feeling strongly that the PLP enhanced both accountability and leadership among participants.

EARLY LESSONS

Signs were abundant in the first implementation sites that the design goals of the PLP were meeting with success. Several of the issues that emerged through examination of these particular sites are discussed.

Implementation in a number of varied sites and contexts confirmed that the structures of the PLP are flexible enough to meet the needs of every permutation of learning community yet encountered. Participants reported high levels of satisfaction with several aspects of the PLP's flexible design, including the easy customization of roles and groups; the ability to develop different sets of standards, goals, rubrics, and surveys for those groups; and the natural affordance of technology to transcend traditional boundaries of distance or time.

The nature of PLP-embedded information about student progress and growth over time provided many learners and advisors with a strong sense of the power of diagnostic assessment of their works-in-progress. They also began to comprehend and value the linkage of their work to personal goals and institutional standards, and the importance of a record of continuity and growth in their learning experiences. In many settings, learning was both supported and extended through the ongoing reflection and dialogue supported by the PLP's structure. However, this complex vision of learning and assessment also accounted for difficulties as well. Many challenges in implementation stemmed from the observed fact that the vision of learning and assessment as a process in addition to a product was difficult for participants at various institutions to incorporate into their practice.

In each of the explored pilot sites, effective program ownership and advocacy to build interest, enthusiasm, and commitment around use of the PLP was perceived as a critical factor supporting implementation. Some sites experienced difficulty stemming from different personnel being responsible for the technical and the conceptual ownership of the PLP at their site. Where these functions were consolidated in one person, that program tended to be successful. In several settings, both users and advisors were less active in their engagement with the PLP until advocates insured that it either became part of their programmatic requirements, or explicitly demonstrated its utility in helping meet their larger personal and professional goals. The presence, commitment, and informed outreach efforts are likely to play a key role in the PLP's future sustainability among existing and new learner communities.

THE PLP AND CULTURAL CHANGE

Perhaps the most powerful and challenging process observed at each of the PLP sites was the intersection of existing cultural norms with some of the changes in thinking and practices implied by the approach to learning, assessment, standards, and mentorship embedded in the PLP. On one level, the importance of considering participants' experience with portfolio systems prior to using the PLP was very evident among the pilot users (cf. Barrett, 1998). In a deeper sense, the cultural or institutional practices and prior experiences of different pilot groups strongly influenced their initial engagements with the PLP. Beyond their experience with paper portfolios, different groups had varying types of norms in place surrounding many aspects of their work with the PLP. This included at various times participant conceptions of mentorship, reflection, the purpose of a portfolio-like collection of work, the relevance of such a portfolio to jobs and careers, the idea of assessment as entailing a fixed-point evaluation of a finished product, and familiarity with and ideas about content standards. As users became more familiar with the PLP, some tentative reconsideration of norms of teaching and learning–visible through more reflective comments, active engagement with PLP work, and descriptions of such changes by program administrators–were evident as risk-taking and experimentation with the PLP was supported and encouraged.

Participants' most effective initial engagements with the PLP–those that led to increased buy-in and participation–centered on aspects of its design that were analogous to structures and practices with which participants were already familiar. Expectations and rewards for participation were tied to existing program structures. All potential users of an innovation need to be persuaded of the viability and relevance of a new way of doing things (cf. Rogers, 1995). In these cases of PLP implementation, the program advocates who recognized a match between points of leverage and existing institutional values and conditions exploited those "selling points." In some cases, this constituted the 4-step work cycle or the survey component; for a group that had more extensive experience linking work to standards, creating standards-linked individual goals was a logical first step.

In each case, the approach to learning, assessment, and collaboration embodied in the PLP and embodied in each institution intersected to create a unique PLP site reflecting those aspects of the PLP approach that most fit the given context for implementation. This is likely to be equally true in other programs with their differences in size, scope, and institutional history. Understanding the relative importance of these contextual factors in other programs may help potential adopters consider the relevance of the PLP to their settings, while also helping to identify areas where leaders may wish to instigate or catalyze cultural and institutional change. In all cases, the PLP fostered conditions of increased accountability for both learners and advisors, to each other as well as to the institutional standards that they were charged with meeting. Through this lens, it will be helpful for new adapters to conceptualize the PLP as a way to reify, enhance, and reflect on institutional norms rather than replace them.

FUTURE DIRECTIONS

We have described the design rationale and early stages of execution of the PLP, or Personal Learning Planner, a Web-based application system designed to provide a flexible environment for standards-based work and mentorship. We have also seen that effective use of the PLP will imply cultural changes for many institutions as they rethink the demanding nature of student-mentor relationships, standards-linked performance, and ongoing documentation of professional learning. As use of the PLP scales to wider audiences, it may be worthwhile to develop tools and protocols to help understand the dimensions that will influence the cultural fit of the PLP with candidate groups of learners.

In their initial forays into the PLP medium, participants rehearsed new norms and conventions for working, interacting, reflecting, and providing feedback to others. Each of these forays resulted in a feedback loop of positive reinforcement that added momentum to leaner participation. In a paradox that is common to many such innovations, to fully achieve maximal learning benefits through the PLP requires an up-front period of investment in which those benefits may not be readily apparent. Several sites have worked with the PLP for a long enough period and in such a way as to foster a self-sustaining critical mass of interest and participation. Part of this success at sustaining early engagements is attributable to the high level of personal support provided to pilot sites by the development team. As use of the PLP expands to a wider audience of learning communities, the team will continue to explore structures and roles that can provide this high level of personalized support and customization on a larger scale. Addressing these issues, and further understanding other keys to achieving high levels of interest and participation, will be a critical part of sustaining the PLP beyond the duration of its initial funding period.

While high standards for education are mandated by accountability legislation, few educators are at present adequately familiar with the standards relevant to their practice to implement them fully. One of the outcomes that PLP participants valued was increased familiarity with these standards–both on the part of learners and their administrators. The linking and goal-setting features of the PLP provide an unprecedented dimension of interactivity to standards, and force consideration of their relevance to one's actual work. As the climate around standards becomes more imperative, the PLP is likely to find new audiences that will further contribute to its sustainability. As a component in pre-service teacher education, the PLP can help future and existing teachers arrive in the workforce well-versed in thinking through the complex interaction of standards with their work, prepared to collaboratively reflect on their importance and attainment, and able to powerfully demonstrate their results.

REFERENCES

Andrews, S., Ducharme, A., & Cox, C. (2003). *Development and use of electronic portfolios in pre-service education*. Paper presented at the annual meeting of the Society for Information Technology in Teacher Education (SITE), March 23-26, Albuquerque, NM.

Barrett, H. (1998). What to consider when planning for electronic portfolios. *Learning & Leading with Technology, 26*(2), 6-10.

Bentley, T. (1999, December 8). Students empowered in Montpelier. [Our Generation page]. *Times Argus Newspaper.*

Carroll, T. (2000, February). *If we didn't have the schools we have today, would we create the schools we have today?* Keynote speech at the American Association for Computers in Education /Society for Information Technology in Teacher Education conference, San Diego, CA.

Friedrichs, A. (2000). *Continuous learning dialogues: An ethnography of personal learning plans' impact on four River High School learners*. Unpublished doctoral dissertation, University of Vermont, Burlington, VT.

Friedrichs, A., & Gibson, D. (2001). Personalization and secondary school renewal. In *Personalized learning*, In J. Dimartino, J. Clarke, & D. Wolk (Eds.),. Lanham, MD: Scarecrow Press.

Gibson, D. (1999). *Mapping the dynamics of change: A complexity theory analysis of innovation in five Vermont high schools*. Unpublished doctoral dissertation, University of Vermont, Burlington, VT.

Gibson, D. (2000). *Complexity theory as a leadership framework*. Montpelier, VT: Vermont Institute for Mathematics, Science, and Technology (VISMT). Retrieved May 1, 2006, from VISMT Web site: http://www.vismt.org/pub/ComplexityandLeadership.pdf

Gibson, D., & Clarke, J. (1999). *Growing towards systemic change*. Providence, RI: Brown University Regional Laboratory.

Moffett, J. (1998). *The universal schoolhouse: Spiritual awakening through education*. Portland, ME: Calendar Island Publishers.

Newmann, F.M., & Wehlage, G.G. (1995). *Successful school restructuring: A report to the public and educators*. University of Wisconsin: Center on Organization and Restructuring.

National Staff Development Council. (2001). *E-Learning for educators*. Oxford, OH: Author.

Rogers, E. (1995). *Diffusion of innovations*. New York: The Free Press.

Shepard, L. (2000). The role of assessment in a learning culture. *Educational Researcher, 29*(7), 4-14.

Sherry, L. (2000). The nature and purpose of online conversations: A brief synthesis of current research. *International Journal of Educational Telecommunications, 6*(1), 19-52.

Sherry, L., & Myers, K. (1998). The dynamics of collaborative design. *IEEE Transactions on Professional Communication, 41*(2), 123-139.

Sherry, L., Tavalin, F., & Billig, S. H. (2000). Good online conversation: Building on research to inform practice. *Journal of Interactive Learning Research, 11*(1), 85-127.

Sherry, L., Billig, S. H., Tavalin, F., & Gibson, D. (2000). New insights on technology adoption in schools. *T.H.E. Journal, 27*(7), 43-46.

Stiggins, R.J. (1997). *Student-centered classroom assessment.* Upper Saddle River, NJ: Merrill, Prentice Hall.

Wiggins, G. (1989). Teaching to the (authentic) test. *Educational Leadership, 46,* 41-46.

doi:10.1300/J025v23n03_04

Linda R. Lisowski
Joseph A. Lisowski
Sherry Nicolia

Infusing Technology into Teacher Education: Doing More with Less

SUMMARY. In our pilot effort to integrate technology meaningfully into the three strands of pre-service teacher education (core courses, education courses, and K-12 field experiences), Links to the Future, a PT3 project in a small, private college, prioritized the issue of educational equity. This paper describes the first efforts of three faculty members to meet the goals of the project, the barriers they encountered, and their strategies for coping with or overcoming the barriers. We found that faculty and student attributes related to project success were flexibility, enthusiasm, and creativity. The lessons learned from the pilot project served as a guide as we worked to systematically integrate technology into all aspects of the teacher education program. doi:10.1300/J025v23n03_05 *[Article copies available for a fee from The Haworth Document Delivery Service:*

LINDA R. LISOWSKI is Associate Professor of Education, Elizabeth City State University, Elizabeth City, NC 27909 (E-mail: lrlisowski@mail.ecsu.edu).
JOSEPH A. LISOWSKI is Professor of English, Elizabeth City State University, Elizabeth City, NC 27909 (E-mail: jalisowski@mail.ecsu.edu).
SHERRY NICOLIA is a Learning Support Teacher, Harborcreek School District, Erie, PA 16504 (E-mail: nicolia@velocity.net).

[Haworth co-indexing entry note]: "Infusing Technology into Teacher Education: Doing More with Less." Lisowski, Linda R., Joseph A. Lisowski, and Sherry Nicolia. Co-published simultaneously in *Computers in the Schools* (The Haworth Press, Inc.) Vol. 23, No. 3/4, 2006, pp. 71-92; and: *Teaching Teachers to Use Technology* (ed: D. LaMont Johnson, and Kulwadee Kongrith) The Haworth Press, Inc., 2006, pp. 71-92. Single or multiple copies of this article are available for a fee from The Haworth Document Delivery Service [1-800-HAWORTH, 9:00 a.m. - 5:00 p.m. (EST). E-mail address: docdelivery@haworthpress.com].

1-800-HAWORTH. E-mail address: <docdelivery@haworthpress.com> Website:
<http://www.HaworthPress.com> © 2006 by The Haworth Press, Inc. All rights
reserved.]

KEYWORDS. Infusing technology, teacher education, PT3, integrate technology

Technology is perceived by many to have tremendous potential to transform school culture (see, for example, Carter & Cunningham, 1997). Federal, state, and local governments have invested millions of dollars to provide school children with computer hardware and software and access to the Internet. And yet many teachers report that they do not often use the technology that they have available to them (Becker, Ravitz, & Wong, 1999). It is a reasonable assumption that teachers are not using technology because they either do not know how to use it, or are not comfortable using it. Many schools, colleges, and departments of education (SCDEs) are addressing this lack of knowledge and comfort through the integration of technology into the teacher-training program. The federal government has played a key role in this initiative through the generous funding of the Preparing Tomorrow's Teachers to Use Technology (PT3) program. We were the recipients of two PT3 grants while at a small private college in the Northeast. We received our first capacity-building grant in 1999 and later received a three-year implementation grant.

VALUES AND GOALS

Like all PT3 projects, Links to the Future was designed to increase our ability to systematically address our use of technology in the teaching/learning process in order to improve the quality of K-12 teaching and learning. We began by first considering what we believe "improved" classrooms would look like. We identified several key, related beliefs that we wanted to incorporate into our project: (a) that educational equity must be a priority in educational reform efforts; (b) that for authentic learning to occur people must take ownership of the process, outcomes, and artifacts of their learning; (c) that current best practice supports the use of technology to enhance active and collaborative student learning of intellectually complex tasks and skills; and (d) that pre-service teachers must see technology used effectively if they are to use it as teachers.

First, we believe that all education reform efforts should address issues of equity. This is certainly true of digital equity, but even more so, we wanted to address the larger issue of educational equity. Access to not only technological resources, but virtually all educational resources is impacted by ethnicity and class membership (Kozol, 1991; Leigh, 1999). For example, as of 1998, only 39% of classrooms in high-poverty schools had computers equipped with Internet access, compared to 74% of the classrooms in richer schools (Lonergan, 2000). We see the digital divide as part of a much larger social justice issue that is a result of socio-economic differences. We wanted to achieve the goals of our project in such a way that it enhanced educational equity for those students who frequently are on the short end of the educational receiving line. Because of this, we found that in many cases our technology resources were limited, and would stay that way for the duration of the project–so we needed to do more with less. Even in urban schools where computers are present, for example, we found that they were often older and slower, with cumbersome connectivity. Because a significant advantage of technology and connectivity is high-speed, what-you-want, when-you-want-it access, cumbersome equipment can negate the appeal and advantage of technology to students (Dede, 1995; Owston, 1997). Our approach to the integration of technology needed to be flexible, appealing to students, and manageable with older equipment. However, we expected that as we made effective use of the available equipment, we would position ourselves to secure more equipment in the future.

In addition to limited hardware resources, we were often working with limited human resources; i.e., tech support and technological expertise. This project took place at a small, private college, located in a small city. We needed to seriously consider the question of how we would learn what we needed to know. Freire's (1998) discussion of fear was especially relevant to us:

If one takes on a [task] whose comprehension will require some work, one needs to know

1. whether one's ability to respond is at the level of the challenge posed . . .
2. whether one's ability to respond is less than is needed to meet the challenge.

3. whether one's ability to respond is more than needed to meet the challenge . . .

> If one's ability to respond is less than needed to meet a given challenge, one must not allow oneself to be immobilized by the fear of not understanding or, by defining the task as impossible to realize, to simply abandon it. If my ability to respond to a [task] is less than is needed . . . , I must seek the help of someone . . . in overcoming at least some of the limitations that make the task more difficult. (p. 28)

And so, we decided to utilize the expertise of others in order to "grow" our own knowledge as our primary strategy for gaining expertise. Access to expertise–who knew what we needed to know, and how could we find them–became an important factor in our project design. Since we didn't have large numbers of people to help us meet the goals of the project, we needed to work in active learning communities, where expertise is shared and leadership roles shift according to the task at hand.

This "limitation" thus worked to support student ownership of the learning, as well as another key belief that we hold: that the infusion of technology into the curriculum is only of value if it supports effective teaching practices. Advocates for both a constructivist model of education and a direct instruction model of education agree on the importance of active student participation and high levels of student engagement in learning tasks (e.g., Brooks & Brooks, 1993; Carnine, Silbert, & Kameenui, 1997). We emphasized the use of active learning, student collaboration, and project-based units, but we maintained a recognition that in inclusive K-12 classrooms, there are students who will require direct instruction in some skills and activities.

We also believe that technology is best used when it increases students' engagement and success with intellectually complex tasks. For example, we see no inherent superiority of a lecture which utilizes a PowerPoint slide show over a lecture that uses overhead transparencies (or the chalkboard, for that matter); and, while computer drill activities are motivating to students and provide opportunities for repetition, increase student time on task, and meet students' individual needs, they limit students to the lower order thinking skills. This is an especially critical issue for students in low socioeconomic schools, because it appears that, in general, they are more likely to be engaged in activities that utilize lower order thinking skills. We wanted our students and teachers to be both actively engaged and intellectually challenged.

Finally, we recognized that the most powerful models of teaching for pre-service teachers come from the teaching that they experience and the teaching they observe. So we utilized a three-strand approach to our project: (a) technology in the core classroom, (b) technology in the educational methods classroom, and (c) technology in the K-12 classroom. In all three strands, we emphasized the attainment of the ISTE, NETS, and Pennsylvania academic standards for pre-service teachers and K-12 students. In the following sections, we discuss sample project activities that occurred across the three strands during the pilot year of the project and that served, along with other activities, to help us pinpoint exactly what we could do well and where we needed to develop expertise. Each project described shares several components. First, all projects chose to utilize PowerPoint as a tool for student learning and as an artifact of that learning; second, all projects experienced barriers, including significant attitudinal and skill barriers and technology barriers; and, third, all projects were able to address the barriers and provide exciting opportunities for learning.

THREE CASES

Core Class–College Writing 102

The second author worked to meet the project goals in his College Writing II course, taught at the branch campus. Students at the branch campus were those students whose scores were not sufficiently high for admission to the main campus. These included many single-parent adult students, minorities, and re-entry women. In many cases, they had not done well in a "traditional" learning environment and harbored a distrust for the process of education. Significant attitudinal problems had to be overcome. In this regard, we considered what Paulo Freire (1998) has said, "To teach is *not to transfer knowledge* but to create the possibilities for the production or construction of knowledge" (p. 30).

The first task for the course was to create an environment of both high expectations and trust. Because this was a writing course, students wrote–frequently and much. Responses to writing prompts–selected because of their relevance to student's lives–were discussed in class and shared in groups. By the end of the third week of class, the class was becoming comfortable with one another and beginning to trust one another. During the fourth week of class students were asked to post their responses to the prompt and to one another's writings on Blackboard. It was at this time that the professor became aware of the first major barrier to the successful attainment of project goals: The computer lab on that campus at the time had only one lab with 12 machines available for student use. We reserved that lab for one college writing class period and students were able to enroll in Blackboard and learn to use the discussion room. On that day only five computers were able to access the Internet. (Since then, the college has significantly improved computer availability, quality, and connectivity.) Nevertheless, the class heeded Blake's Proverb "If a fool persists in his folly, he will become wise"–and persisted in the task. Within two days, most students had been able to post their entries.

Next, students were asked to comment on at least two postings. This had a dramatic effect on how each student prepared copy to be posted. Much more care was taken with grammar, spelling, and sentence construction. The content of the responses, too, improved noticeably–students more frequently wrote about their own similar personal experiences. The sharing process had begun in earnest. Students found value in the exchanges and took more care in their presentations. While a new level of trust was developing, problems with computers available on campus skyrocketed. The computers often did not have enough memory to complete the simple function of pasting a 350-word document from a floppy to Blackboard. Still, the students persevered. At that time, about half the students had access to computers outside the computer lab. This percentage increased as students became more known to one another and willing to share resources. They liked "talking" to one another on the Net, and, as a result, were writing more lengthy pieces with more care.

With a high level of trust established, the class turned its attention to research. Five groups of students were to research some very specific aspect of life in the college town. As is appropriate in constructivist classrooms, the students' interests and needs would be of primary concern in the development and evaluation of the project (Brooks & Brooks, 1993). Each group would decide what they wanted to know, how they would go about finding the information, how they would divide up the workload. The professor required that each group publicly present its findings in a PowerPoint presentation utilizing graphics, sound, and text. After about 10 minutes of distress, the class began to address the project constructively. Five students who had done PowerPoint previously felt comfortable being group leaders. Students determined to which group they wanted to belong with the stipulation that all groups needed five to seven members. Class time was used to decide research topics.

Through PT3 grant resources, each group was able to borrow a digital camera for a "one day rental." The groups could "renew" the rental, if there wasn't a "hold" on it. Each week, groups reported their progress and used 10 minutes of each scheduled class for group meetings. Although the computers on campus were inadequate for the tasks, in each group there was at least one student who had access to a computer adequate for the project needs. Within a month, each group was well on its way to producing a finished product; each was enthusiastic about what the group was doing; and members of various groups often shared their "expertise" with others if they needed it. The class set a presentation date.

What remained was the determination of criteria to evaluate the end result. What specific items would be assessed? As a large group they brainstormed, coming up with about 15 categories. Unanimous consent was required. No item would be part of the grade checklist unless everyone agreed on it. The class discussed and agreed upon five criteria–Clarity of Main Point (Focus); Composition–(balance of text, graphics, and sound); Organization and Flow; Creativity; and Fitting Conclusion–to be accompanied by half a page of verbal comments. Two suggestions the professor made and put on the board for discussion were not accepted. Clearly, the students had taken full ownership of their work; the professor was not the only authority; he was simply another member of the group who may have had some good points but whose opinions did not override those of class members. To enhance their critical evaluation skills, all students would evaluate the other group presentations. Student evaluations were used to determine a group project grade; however, the professor maintained final responsibility for the grading process.

As it turned out, the students' presentations were outstanding. The students demonstrated significant attainment of two of the National Educational Technology Standards for Teachers: Teachers demonstrate a sound understanding of technology operations and concepts (standard I); and teachers use technology to enhance their productivity and professional practice (standard V). In addition, the professor modeled and the students demonstrated strong attainment of the standard addressing social, ethical, and human issues, specifically, standard VI-B: apply technology resources to enable and empower learners with diverse backgrounds, characteristics, and abilities (International Society for Technology in Education, 2000). The immediate effect of the project was that now each member of the class addressed the issue of research in a more personal and dynamic way. They had not been overcome by fear. They had used technology to take ownership of their learning, to commit themselves to an intellectually demanding and frustrating task, and to take justifiable pride in their efforts. They then were able to use this vital and interactive approach for the remaining classroom tasks.

Educational Methods Class–Teaching Students with Physical Disabilities

The first author worked to meet the project goals in a required methods course for graduate special education and dual special education/elementary education certification students. Teaching Students with Physical Disabilities is a course designed to insure that students who receive Pennsylvania's non-categorical special education certificate have experience and skills related to the needs of students with orthopedic and health impairments. The course used Blackboard for posting course information and documents, linking to critical readings, and communicating among class members. At the time of this pilot project, the first author had a graduate assistant with a rare form of muscular dystrophy who served as a teaching assistant for the course. Because of her high level of independence and her limited movement abilities (she has use of two fingers in her right hand, along with adequate head control), this graduate assistant also provided the class members with a powerful example of the need for them to develop advanced computer skills if they were to teach young students with serious orthopedic impairments.

Students in the graduate program had varied backgrounds. They included certified special educators, certified elementary teachers, uncertified paraprofessionals in education and mental health fields, younger students straight from their undergraduate programs, and re-entry women with family and other work experiences. Many students were highly anxious about beginning a new mid-life career. Others were young and intimidated by the experiences of the older students. Yet all of the students brought personal and professional strengths to the class. Planning and delivering instruction so that all students' strengths were utilized and all students' needs were met were often significant challenges. Collaborative, project-based learning was seen as a way to utilize strengths and meet needs in this kind of diverse setting.

For their final project of the course, students were asked to work in self-selected small groups to develop either a Web-based or PowerPoint instructional unit (all students elected to do PowerPoint), saved on a CD-ROM, and designed to meet the needs of students with average cognitive skills utilizing the principles of universal design. That is, the instructional unit needed to be barrier-free to meet the needs of students with physical impairments, but still had to be of interest to students with no visual, hearing, or physical impairments. The project was designed to enable students to demonstrate growth in or attainment of the National Educational Technology Standards for Teachers (International Society for Technology in Education, 2000).

The grading checklist included six areas upon which students work would be graded:

1. Learning objectives are clear, appropriate to the grade level and content area, and identified within the first two "pages" of the presentation;
2. Content is accurate and appropriately challenging;
3. Users can choose whether to access the unit visually and/or auditorily, and the unit is clear and cohesive in either modality;
4. There are at least three to four high-quality Internet links embedded in the unit;
5. The unit includes an assessment component that precisely matches learning objectives and content; and
6. The appearance and appeal of the unit are high.

Students were free to select the grade level and content area of the unit.

In selecting groups, students needed to consider geographical access: many students commuted from up to 40 miles away. In addition, they were encouraged to work in groups in which at least one member had technological self-confidence and access to a good computer. However, Links to the Future provided two laptops for students to borrow (one PC and one Mac), if they needed. Students could also borrow portable zip drives (to facilitate working between computers), digital cameras and video cameras, microphones, and a rewritable CD burner. In addition, graduate assistants staffed a small lab that had two high performance computers, a scanner, and other peripheral equipment. The graduate assistants were available, by appointment, to meet with students and provide technological support, as was the professor.

The first barrier to the successful completion of this project was attitudinal. It would not be too strong a statement to say that many students were horrified and angry when they first received the assignment. They had strong misgivings about their ability to complete the task, and many felt that it was an inappropriate task to be given in a non-computer course. However, they could clearly perceive that students with physical disabilities need excellent technology skills if they are to have access to educational resources and learning; and, given promises of support, they agreed to work beyond their own misgivings and fears. Here it was important that an atmosphere of trust had been previously established. The professor and graduate assistants worked hard to maintain that trust by listening carefully to student concerns and by providing technological assistance. Nonetheless, during the time students were working on the assignment, there were many expressions of frustration and resistance; there were far fewer expressions of excitement and enthusiasm.

The second barrier involved selection of group members. Students needed to balance their own areas of curricular interest (science, math, social studies, etc.) and grade level (preschool, primary, intermediate, middle, or high). They needed to find someone who had a computer and was confident of his/her ability to use it and, perhaps more importantly, play with it. Finally, they needed to find group members who lived or worked within a reasonable distance of one another. With school, work, and family responsibilities to balance, these students were not available to meet on campus regularly. They needed to meet at one other's homes and schools, as well. And, of course, as is always the case in collaborations, they needed other group members they could trust to carry a fair share of the work burden. In spite of geographical and technological barriers, almost all group members rose to the challenge and worked together effectively, meeting their own responsibilities and supporting one another. One group of three students was unable to develop a strong working relationship, and members did not trust each other to complete tasks. This problem was exacerbated by family problems one member was experiencing at the time. However, this group requested an extension on the due date and was eventually able to resolve their issues and complete the project satisfactorily.

The third barrier to the success of the project involved technology. Group members struggled with compatibility of software and hardware. Often work had to be redone as students discovered that work completed on one version of an application program could not be read by another version. Several students attempted, for the first time, to do tasks that exceeded the memory capability of their computers. An especially distressing glitch occurred with several groups. After completing the project and saving their work onto a CD-ROM, they found that they had not saved file extensions along with their work, and were unable to play the CD on any computer but the one on which they had initially constructed their presentation. With patience, humor, and hard work, these barriers were overcome.

Students presented their projects during the final week of classes. They ranged from a simple math fact unit for first-graders to an interactive intermediate grade unit on the Bill of Rights to a richly informative unit on Chinese life and culture. Some of the presentations were of outstanding quality-class members were astounded by the interesting presentations that the groups developed. In spite of the anxiety and dread the project engendered while students were working on it, the end result was unquestionably positive. Students who had complained the loudest commented on what a powerful and positive learning experience this assignment had provided them.

Field Experiences in the K-12 Classroom

The third author furthered the goals of the project by establishing contact with a first-year teacher instructing in an impoverished, inner city, high-minority population school. One of the Links to the Future assumptions is that there is little point instructing our pre-service teachers how to use and integrate technology into the classroom unless they have the opportunity to practice using it in an actual classroom setting: "pre-service teachers who (1) observed their instructors model technology integration, (2) were required to develop technology-rich lesson/unit plans, and (3) completed several assignments using technology were extremely positive about the use of technology" (Vannatta & Beyerbach, 2000, p. 133). Another assumption is that we could mutually benefit our pre-service teachers and at-risk K-12 students. The pre-service teachers would benefit by seeing and practicing integrating technology in the classroom, while the K-12 students would begin to gain technology and writing skills as required by Pennsylvania's state standards in reading, writing, and speaking (see Appendix A), and the national technology standards (International Society for Technology in Education, 2000) (see Appendix B). With this project there was also the added benefit of supporting a beginning teacher who was eager to try integrating technology into the curriculum.

The project itself was the culmination of a three-month long unit on Ancient Rome and Ancient Greece. Each of the sixth-grade students was to create a PowerPoint presentation outlining at least three different similarities and differences between the two cultures. The pre-service teachers were to act as support for the students by guiding research using trade books and Internet resources and by helping with any questions that the students may have had about creating the PowerPoint. When the project began, the students had one Mac computer in their classroom, which had Internet access. In addition, the school had a Mac computer lab with 23 computers, all with Internet access.

This project faced many barriers to its successful completion. The first was the low skill level of the sixth-grade students. Many of the students in the class were below grade level in reading and comprehension skills, which made it difficult for them to complete the research and compile it into a usable format. Therefore, the students would require extra time and close supervision in order to complete the project. This factor was compounded by the students' limited access to computers and lack of computer skills. In their classroom, there was only one Internet-capable computer, so the teacher had to rely on the computer lab, which was scheduled by other classes throughout most of the day. The project would work only if other teachers did not utilize their scheduled times in the computer room. Since the whole school used these machines, there were also problems with memory and freezing, as well as scheduling conflicts. This led to the need for planning flexibility. When possible, pre-service teachers volunteered to come in at other than their set time to aid students in researching at the computer lab, only to become frustrated by the technological problems mentioned earlier. Fortunately, toward the end of the project, 10 laptop computers were purchased for the school. This meant that, although the Internet still could not be accessed in the classroom, the students could work on the PowerPoint aspect of the project in their own classroom during times that were convenient for them and their teacher, supported by the pre-service teachers.

Even though there were barriers to overcome, there were also many positives going for the project. The first was motivation. The classroom teacher was very positive and open to the challenge of integrating technology. Her determination and excitement motivated her students to become energized about learning and completing the project. This positive environment also created a high comfort level for pre-service teachers in which to learn and grow their technological expertise. Another positive of the project was the teacher's knowledge of her students' learning needs and strengths. Of all the barriers, the low skill level of the students was the hardest to overcome. The teacher was able to address this through the materials she made available to the students and through her structuring of the project. First, she provided an abundance of trade books at differing reading levels, and with many pictures, maps, and illustrations. Secondly, she organized the project into small, manageable pieces so that it would be less overwhelming to the students. The teacher started by reviewing how to use a Venn diagram with the students to compare the two cultures. From there, the students re-searched three areas of interest from their Venn Diagrams via the Internet and trade books. This information was then transferred onto a pre-formatted outline to keep the information and sources organized. Once organized, the sixth-grade students created their presentation in PowerPoint using their outline and grading checklist as guides (see Appendix C). The PowerPoint included an introduction, title, summary, and reference slide as well as the slides that compared and contrasted the Ancient Greek and Ancient Roman cultures. Lastly, having the extra support of the pre-service teachers allowed those students who needed more individualized help to get it without taking time away from other areas of the curriculum.

By far the biggest success of this class project was that these students, who normally avoided school work because of its difficulty for them, eagerly took ownership and pride in their learning. In the end, they were pulling teachers and administrators out of the hallway and inviting their parents to view the project they created. The sixth-grade students left this project with not only new skills and a greater knowledge of Ancient Greece and Ancient Rome, but pride in their accomplishments and a new-found appreciation for learning. The pre-service teachers, who were admittedly worried about using technology in the classroom, walked away with a new enthusiasm and fervor about how the computer can be a motivating force in classroom learning with students who are at risk for school failure. The teacher came away from this project with parent and administrative admiration, the knowledge that the students will remember the learning, and an even greater appreciation for the motivating force that technology can be in the classroom.

DISCUSSION

Links to the Future was a PT3 project designed to systematically ad-dress the ability of pre-service teachers to integrate technology into the teaching/learning process. In this project, we attempted to address is-sues of educational equity by providing high-quality learning opportu-nities for pre-service teachers and their K-12 students. We encouraged active, project-based student collaborations with emphasis on the analy-sis, synthesis, and evaluation of information. Believing that the effec-tive integration of technology into the pre-service teacher course of study can significantly impact students' skill level, attitudes toward technology, and use of technology in their own classrooms (Abbott &

Faris, 2000; Halpin, 1999), this project worked to enhance technology integration across the core curriculum, education methods courses, and K-12 field experiences. Links to the Future pilot projects that were successful in the three cases described here each experienced significant barriers to their success, and each was able to overcome or cope with those barriers sufficiently so that high-quality learning opportunities were provided for all participants.

Barriers and Successes

The first barrier that each project faced was attitudinal and skill related. Most students and pre-service teachers had limited technology skills and confidence regarding their own use of technology; some had limited literacy and academic skills; and some disliked and had high levels of anxiety about tasks that were intellectually challenging. Freire's words (1998) become especially relevant here. If students are to overcome their fears and anxieties, they must first recognize what they are capable of doing, and they must then obtain the assistance of others to do what they are not capable of doing alone. It was critical to the success of these projects that an atmosphere of trust had been established previously. This allowed students to take the risk inherent in admitting that they did not possess the skills necessary to complete an assignment, and to have confidence that the admission will carry no penalty, either academic or social. Risk-taking was therefore another attribute that these successful project participants shared.

A second barrier was adequate technology resources. This was a problem that we recognized would be an issue from the start. We deliberately chose to work with groups of students whose access to technology was limited. For example, the college chose to partner with an urban school district with limited technology and connectivity rather than with a technology-rich suburban school district. We found that, locally, suburban students were already receiving a technology-integrated curriculum. We wanted to apply our efforts where we felt we could have the most impact. Because of our limited technology resources, students and teachers (K-12 and college) were required to be flexible and creative in their scheduling, as well as in their completion of project tasks. This was an essential element in the success of all the projects. Along with flexibility, teacher enthusiasm was important in conveying to students a sense of the potential sheer fun of the project. In general, those students who brought a sense of playfulness and a willingness to take risks to the project were able to develop more interesting presentations.

For example, in the college writing course, one group's presentation called "High Life" investigated the ironies of campus life. In it, one photo clip showed two girls in the girls' dormitory bathroom. Both, looking over their shoulders and mugging for the camera, stood in front of urinals. In the physical disabilities methods class, a particularly playful project allowed the students to learn about the Bill of Rights by donning a detective hat and solving cases that practiced their knowledge and understanding of the first 10 amendments of the U. S. Constitution. The premise of the project was to motivate students to seek knowledge and understanding about the Bill of Rights by integrating the learning into an enjoyable, yet educational activity where they could also practice their intuitive and problem-solving skills. The goal of the unit was to capture "Mr. Wrong" and recover the Bill of Rights.

While attitudes were important in overcoming technology barriers, they were not sufficient. In addition, Links to the Future provided portable equipment that project participants could borrow on an as-needed (and only when-needed) basis. Strict records needed to be kept in order to insure that equipment didn't get borrowed, and not returned. The extra work involved in accounting for equipment and the risks of damage or loss, however, paled in comparison to the benefits it provided students. The college and school districts also allocated resources toward the purchase of new, high-end equipment when they saw that the current equipment was being used beyond its capacity. This willingness to reallocate resources to technology was critical to the success of the project.

An additional component of two of the projects was the requirement that students work collaboratively in groups. This component became both a barrier and a strength of the projects. The K-12 field experience did not require student collaboration. That teacher normally had provided many opportunities for students to work collaboratively, but believed strongly that for this project her students needed to demonstrate their knowledge, skills, and abilities individually. Nonetheless, they had frequent opportunities to work together in the gathering of information, and were frequently observed huddled over each other's computer screens reading presentations, giving feedback and support, and providing assistance. The two college-level courses did require students to work in groups. Barriers to success involved the difficulty that adult students may have in creating time for group projects. Adult students balance work, school, and family responsibilities. These responsibilities often leave little time available to schedule additional meetings with others. For example, a single working mother might find the only time available to her to work on a project is after 11 pm. This time would not be suitable for meeting with group members, however. And more responsible members of the group may carry an unfair portion of the group's workload. This was a significant concern in the development of the projects; nonetheless, we left it as a requirement because of our belief in the value of student collaborations.

We believe that through collaboration individual students are best able to present, test, refine, and augment their perceptions. Not only are individual skills dramatically sharpened but the reality of a shared "life" encourages curiosity, tolerance, and social responsibility. Individually, many students possessed neither the skills nor the technology to complete their projects. They required the abilities and resources of each member of the group to succeed. These resources often were found in unexpected places. For example, one group was able to learn what they needed to know from the young teen-age children of one of the group members. Beyond the discovery that technology *is* used in the K-12 classroom, the discovery that their children knew so much more than they did was a strong motivation to learn! Other groups relied on husbands, wives, and parents. Because this assistance came on a what-we-need, when-we-need-it basis, it was much more powerful than the assistance that was provided in formal class sessions. In fact, we perceived this what-we-need, when-we-need-it type of assistance as so critical that we formalized it in our later projects.

A final component of all three projects that served to enhance the success of the project and limit the barriers was the use of explicit criteria for task definition and evaluation. Because of the increasing amounts of information available today, it is no longer appropriate to require students to simply gather information; critical evaluation has become essential (Grabe & Grabe, 1998). In all of the projects discussed, students were required not only to gather information from multiple sources, but to critically analyze it, synthesize it, and create a new source of information for others to then use. Rubrics and checklists made explicit to students the standards for the task and demystify the grading process. This served to alleviate student anxiety about both task definition and grading. Whether the checklist was developed by the students themselves or by the class teacher, their use provided a clear road map as to where student energies should be focused, where creativity and innovation were appropriate, and where students needed to pay strict attention to requirements. Students developed the capacity to evaluate their own work; they were encouraged and challenged in their efforts to learn and grow; and their abilities to think critically were enhanced.

Lessons Learned

Our beginning efforts to integrate technology into teacher education provided us with valuable lessons as we planned ways to build upon our limited successes to fully "prepare tomorrow's teachers to use technology." The first lesson we learned was that students and adults will need significant amounts of support as they first utilize technology in ways that genuinely enhance learning. The second lesson was more problematic for us, given our deeply held beliefs about the importance of educational equity: In order for pre-service teachers to use technology effectively, a functioning technology infrastructure must be in place.

As college faculty members who were not technology experts, we had been using technology at work and home since the late 1980s. We hardly considered ourselves cutting edge. However, it quickly became clear to us that more than 15 years after computers became affordable and popular for home use, many of our students (especially our non-traditional students) had very little experience with technology. Their lack of experience seemed to breed a lack of confidence that in some cases seemed close to panic. It was clear to us that some students would need a level of support that we could not give, at least not while meeting our other professional responsibilities. (We think it worth noting here that some of our current non-traditional students still approach technology with high levels of anxiety.) At the same time that we were surprised by students' lack of confidence, we were impressed with their abilities to utilize technology in ways that genuinely enhanced the quality of their own and their students' learning when they had the needed support and instruction. For this reason, during the second phase of the project, we hired graduate students who would serve as mentors to our participants.

Technology mentors were available by appointment and during office hours to meet with any faculty member or student who required assistance in using technology. Mentors were careful not to "do" technology for others, but rather to talk them through the steps, and to provide written directions when appropriate. Faculty members who so requested had a mentor assigned to them, and that mentor worked regularly with the faculty member to help meet the faculty member's own technology goals. This what-we-need, when-we need-it training component later proved to be the most successful aspect of our project.

Our second lesson was not so easily learned. Because we place such a high value on educational equity, we chose to work with an urban rather than a suburban school district. However, the district had limited resources and was facing strong pressures to more directly address the needs of its students for enhanced reading and mathematics instruction. In the face of these pressures, technology was seen as a luxury-desirable, but not strictly essential. Given the purpose of the PT3 project, and our knowledge that students learn best by doing and that time on task is critical to effective learning, we finally determined that we were providing a disservice to our pre-service teachers by placing them in settings where significant amounts of learning time were spent trying to get the limited technology to work. Eventually, and with some distress, the project directors decided to end our partnership with the urban school district and create a new partnership with a technology-rich suburban district. While we no longer provided a direct service to urban K-12 students, we believe we indirectly better served them in the long run through better prepared future teachers. We leave it to our former students to advocate for equitable resources in the schools in which they are now teaching.

In our pilot effort to integrate technology meaningfully into aspects of pre-service teacher education, individual Links to the Future projects experienced several barriers to success. However, these barriers did not prove to be insurmountable as project participants (faculty and students, K-12 and college) demonstrated flexibility, creativity, and enthusiasm. The lessons learned from the project served as a guide as we worked to integrate technology into *all* aspects of our teacher education program.

REFERENCES

Abbott, J. A., & Faris, S. E. (2000). Integrating technology into preservice literacy instruction: A survey of elementary education students' attitudes toward computers. *Journal of Research on Computing in Education, 33*(2), 149-161.

Becker, H. J., Ravitz, J. L., & Wong, Y. (1999). Teacher and teacher-directed use of computers and software: Teaching, learning, and computing. *1998 National Survey Report #3.* Irvine, CA, and Minneapolis, MN: Center for Research on Information Technology and Organizations, University of California, Irvine, and University of Minnesota.

Brooks, J. G., & Brooks, M. G. (1993). *The case for constructivist classrooms.* Alexandria, VA: Association for Supervision and Curriculum Development.

Carnine, D. W., Silbert, J., & Kameenui, E. J. (1997) *Direct instruction reading* (3rd Ed.). Upper Saddle River, NJ: Merrill.

Carter, G., & Cunningham, W. (1997). *The American school superintendent: Leading in an age of pressure.* San Francisco: Jossey-Bass.

Dede, C. (1995). The evolution of constructivist learning environments: Immersion in distributed, virtual worlds. *Educational Technology, 35*(5), 46-52.

Freire, P. (1998). *Teachers as cultural workers: Letters to those who dare teach.* Boulder, CO: Westview Press.

Grabe, M., & Grabe, C. (1998). *Integrating technology for meaningful learning.* Boston: Houghton-Mifflin.

Halpin, R. (1999). A model of constructivist learning in practice: Computer literacy integrated into elementary mathematics and science teacher education. *Journal of Research on Computing in Education, 32(*1), 128-131.

International Society for Technology in Education. (2000). National educational standards for students. Retrieved October 15, 2001 from http://cnets.iste.org/sfors.htm.

International Society for Technology in Education. (2000). National educational standards for teachers. Retrieved October 15, 2001 from http://cnets.iste.org/teachstandintro.html

Kozol, J. (1991). *Savage inequalities: Children in America's schools.* New York: Crown Publishers.

Leigh, P. R. (1999). Electronic connections and equal opportunities: An analysis of telecommunications distribution in public schools. *Journal of Research on Computing in Education, 32*(1), 108-127.

Lonergan, J. M. (2000). Internet access and content for urban schools and communities (ERIC Digest Number 157). New York: ERIC Clearinghouse on Urban Education.

Owston, R. D. (1997). The World Wide Web: A technology to enhance teaching and learning. *Educational Researcher, 26*(2), 27-33.

Vannatta, R. A., & Beyerbach, B. (2000). Facilitating a constructivist vision of technology integration among education faculty and pre-service teachers. *Journal of Research on Computing in Education, 33*(2), 132-148.

doi:10.1300/J025v23n03_05

APPENDIX A
Pennsylvania Standards in Reading, Writing, and Speaking
Addressed in K-12 Research Project

1.8 Research

1.8.5.

A. Select and refine a topic for research.

B. Locate information using appropriate sources and strategies.
  - Evaluate the usefulness and qualities of the sources.
  - Select appropriate sources (e.g., dictionaries, encyclopedias, other reference materials, interviews, observations, computer databases).
  - Use tables of contents, indices, key words, cross-references, and appendices.
  - Use traditional and electronic search tools.

C. Organize and present the main ideas from research.
  - Take notes from sources using a structured format.
  - Present the topic using relevant information.
  - Credit sources using a structured format (e.g., author, title).

1.6 Speaking and Listening

1.6.8.

F. Use media for learning purposes.
  - Describe how the media provides information that is sometimes accurate, sometimes biased based on a point of view or by the opinion or beliefs of the presenter.
  - Analyze the role of advertising in the media.
  - Create a multimedia (e.g., film, music, computer-graphic) presentation for display or transmission.

APPENDIX B
ISTE Standards Achieved in the K-12 Research Project

NT.K-12.1 Basic Operations and Concepts
- Students demonstrate a sound understanding of the nature and operation of technology systems.
- Students are proficient in the use of technology.

NT.K-12.3 Technology Productivity Tools
- Students use technology tools to enhance learning, increase productivity, and promote creativity.
- Students use productivity tools to collaborate in constructing technology-enhanced models, prepare publications, and produce other creative works.

NT.K-12.4 Technology Communication Tools
- Students use telecommunications to collaborate, publish, and interact with peers, experts, and other audiences.
- Students use a variety of media and formats to communicate information and ideas effectively to multiple audiences.

NT.K-12.5 Technology Research Tools
- Students use technology to locate, evaluate, and collect information from a variety of sources.
- Students use technology tools to process data and report results.
- Students evaluate and select new information resources and technological innovations based on the appropriateness for specific tasks.

APPENDIX C
Compare and Contrast Grade Checklist

Critical Components

*Contains three elements to compare/contrast
*Contains an introduction, body, conclusion, reference, and title page
*Introduction clearly states reason for writing
*Conclusion summarizes body
*Body includes likes and differences of each chosen aspect
*Each paragraph is supported by facts

Style

Word Choice
*uses strong active verbs
*uses precise words
*includes adjectives to add interest
*uses writing devices, such as metaphors to get meaning across
Coherence
*Clearly presented ideas
*Logically sequenced
*pictures added for clarity
Originality
*Colorful and eye pleasing
Mechanics
*Ending punctuation present
*capitalization for proper nouns and at the beginning of sentences
*Follows comma rules
*Uses quotation marks when someone is speaking
*Paragraph is correctly structured
*References are correctly formatted

Wayne A. Nelson
Melissa Thomeczek

Design as a Focus
for Technology Integration:
Lessons Learned from a PT3 Project

SUMMARY. The Plugging in to L.I.T.E.S. project (Leaders in Technology Enhanced Schools–a previously funded Technology Innovation Challenge grant project) at Southern Illinois University Edwardsville (SIUE) has been very successful in its attempts to enhance the technology integration skills of teacher education students, and to improve the capabilities of our faculty members to provide effective modeling of technology integration strategies. This was accomplished through the use of professional development activities focused on design tasks, and the use of a "design studio" metaphor to organize and promote the redesign of our curriculum to align with the Illinois Core Technology Standards required of all newly certified teachers. To further the technology integration skills of our teacher candidates, partnerships were established with 25 school districts in our service area where many L.I.T.E.S.-trained mentor teachers work, and teacher candidates rotated through

WAYNE A. NELSON is Chairman, Department of Educational Leadership, Southern Illinois University, Edwardsville, IL 62026 (E-mail: wnelson@siue.edu).
MELISSA THOMECZEK is Assistant Professor of Instructional Technology, Department of Educational Leadership, Southern Illinois University, Edwardsville, IL 62026 (E-mail: mthomec@siue.edu).

[Haworth co-indexing entry note]: "Design as a Focus for Technology Integration: Lessons Learned from a PT3 Project." Nelson, Wayne A., and Melissa Thomeczek. Co-published simultaneously in *Computers in the Schools* (The Haworth Press, Inc.) Vol. 23, No. 3/4, 2006, pp. 93-104; and: *Teaching Teachers to Use Technology* (ed: D. LaMont Johnson, and Kulwadee Kongrith) The Haworth Press, Inc., 2006, pp. 93-104. Single or multiple copies of this article are available for a fee from The Haworth Document Delivery Service [1-800-HAWORTH, 9:00 a.m. - 5:00 p.m. (EST). E-mail address: docdelivery@haworthpress.com].

Available online at http://cits.haworthpress.com
doi:10.1300/J025v23n03_06

these schools in a two-year, field-based teacher education program that emphasized technology integration. In addition, a comprehensive online resource was designed to explicate the state's technology standards for students and to assist them in the development of electronic portfolios that demonstrate their technology integration competencies. To date, more than 800 teacher education students have been supported in their efforts to plan and implement instructional practices that effectively integrate technology. The lessons learned through this project will hopefully provide guidance to those involved with technology integration in teacher education programs. doi:10.1300/J025v23n03_06 *[Article copies available for a fee from The Haworth Document Delivery Service: 1-800-HAWORTH. E-mail address: <docdelivery@haworthpress.com> Website: <http://www.HaworthPress.com> © 2006 by The Haworth Press, Inc. All rights reserved.]*

KEYWORDS. Teacher preparation, technology integration, certification standards, professional development

Southern Illinois University Edwardsville (SIUE) has been very successful in its attempts to enhance the technology integration skills of teacher education candidates through activities intended to revise and improve our approach in three major areas. First, we have sought to improve the abilities of our faculty members to effectively model technology integration strategies through extensive professional development efforts. These efforts, organized around a metaphor of the "design studio" (Rieber, 2000), have resulted in significant revisions to curriculum brought about through collaborations between faculty in the School of Education and the College of Arts and Sciences. Second, we challenged our teacher candidates completing field experiences at partnership sites (with the support of partnership mentor teachers and university faculty) to design and implement learning activities for the classrooms where they were observing or teaching. The success of these efforts was greatly enhanced by the involvement of L.I.T.E.S. teachers who conducted the "design studios" for our teacher candidates and their mentor teachers. Finally, we developed a very comprehensive set of content resources and electronic portfolio tools to support our teacher candidates as they demonstrated and documented the various ways they prepared to meet the state technology standards. Again, design tasks were featured; this time with student design artifacts displayed in electronic portfolios, along with reflections on the outcomes of implementing their designs in classrooms.

BACKGROUND AND ORIGINS

Since 1990, the School of Education at SIUE has implemented an integrated technology curriculum that is designed to provide prospective teachers with necessary experiences and skills that help them effectively utilize technology in the teaching process (Nelson, Andris, & Keefe, 1991). More recently, we were involved with the Illinois State Board of Education's Area 5 Learning Technology Hub in a Technology Innovation Challenge Grant that prepared more than 200 teachers per year to become Leaders In Technology Enhanced Schools (L.I.T.E.S.) teachers. A consortium of schools, Regional Offices of Education, businesses, and the Learning Technology Hub provided participating teachers with holistic professional development "kits" that helped teachers learn to use technology in ways that enhanced, facilitated, and improved teaching and learning in order for students to achieve high academic standards. The teachers participating in the L.I.T.E.S. grant stood ready to act as exemplary models and mentors for teacher education students at SIUE.

At the inception of our PT3 grant, the teacher education programs at SIUE met the standards proposed by ISTE and NCATE, but in 2000 the Illinois State Board of Education announced that new certification standards for teacher education would be required and tested beginning in 2003. Along with standards for content area knowledge and teaching competencies, 49 performance indicators related to 8 general standards for technology skills were required of all newly certified teachers in the state of Illinois (Illinois State Board of Education, 2003). In addition, efforts to comprehensively restructure teacher education programs at SIUE were implemented through Professional Development School (PDS) models beginning in 1999. PDS partnerships with local districts trained teacher education students in a two-year on-site program that was completely integrated within the activities of the schools.

Given this background, we identified several needs that remained as our PDS programs were expanded to include new partnerships with schools in our service area. Results of our analysis of survey, interview, and observation data showed that participation by faculty members in the existing technology integration activities was about 33%, with less participation by faculty in the College of Arts and Sciences who teach courses taken by education students. Likewise, cooperating teachers who mentor student teachers were not aware of the new standards, nor did they consistently model effective technology-based learning activities. It was clear from these results that expanded involvement by university faculty members was necessary to assure that the integrated technology curriculum continued to meet the certification standards set by the state.

Examination of syllabi and interviews with faculty indicated that levels of technology skills among faculty were inconsistent, that there was inconsistent use of integrated technology-based learning activities in courses, and that there were no consistent models employed for planning integrated technology-based learning experiences. It was clear that faculty needed to become proficient in planning effective learning activities that integrate technology, and in modeling appropriate teaching strategies for such activities.

PROJECT ACTIVITIES AND OUTCOMES

Given the results of our needs assessment and the identification of opportunities for change, objectives for the project were established as follows: (a) effective modeling of technology integration by faculty; (b) increased collaboration between teacher candidates and mentor teachers in local schools in utilizing effective technology integration strategies with K-12 students; and (c) increased opportunities for efficient content delivery, communication, and reflection related to the new Illinois Core Technology Standards. Activities related to each of these components of our PT3 project will be described in detail, along with a rationale for choosing the particular strategies that focused on design activities.

Why Design Studios?

Design is increasingly being seen as an activity that can be used to facilitate learning in a variety of content areas and contexts (Perkins, 1986). Design tasks support a kind of learning-on-demand environment, where learning goals emerge from the situation at hand, rather than being contrived by a teacher and presented through an artificial context (Nelson, 2003). Designers collaborate in diverse ways during design tasks and often are required to reflect on where they are and where they are going. As a result, new opportunities for inquiry, participation, and conversation occur as the design process unfolds. From students learning through the design and production of multimedia (e.g., Kahn & Taber Ullah, 1998) to students learning science by constructing and testing solutions to problems (e.g., Harel & Papert, 1991), project-based and problem-based learning that incorporates design tasks has become an effective model for promoting learning.

To organize and manage learning-by-design activities, educators have adopted the model of design studios common in the practices of the visual arts, architecture, and other fields that emphasize design (Orey, Rieber, King, & Matzko, 2000). Studios provide an open learning environment where participants use design tools and processes to complete various real-world–and often self-selected–projects. In most studios, participants make regularly scheduled presentations of their work in progress. These presentations allow participants to give one another suggestions and constructive criticisms of the design process and resulting artifacts. This collaborative atmosphere lends itself well to the self-organized and self-paced learning that occurs in studio design activities (Koehler & Mishra, 2005). The instructor of a design studio acts more as a facilitator and expert designer than an authoritarian giver of knowledge (Rieber, 2000). The facilitator can also moderate peer critiques, where participants offer feedback to their peers. When asked, the facilitator may even offer assistance and critique.

Faculty Technology Design Studios

To help meet the project objectives, we initiated two "technology design studios," one for university faculty members, and one for SIUE teacher candidates and select mentor teachers from the partnership schools where teacher candidates complete their programs. In the faculty technology design studio, 39 faculty members collaborated to design technology-based learning activities that were implemented in courses or field experiences. Eight facilitators with extensive experience in technology integration worked with the faculty groups to assist in the process. After specifying the learning activities, faculty members were assisted in the development of necessary materials and technologies by project staff. Faculty members then implemented the activities, and reported the results to project staff. Qualitative evaluation data collected through surveys indicated that the faculty members appreciated the individualized and collaborative nature of this approach to faculty development. Because faculty members were mentored in these efforts by highly experienced facilitators, and supported by project staff during the subsequent development of electronic materials and resources, the technology-related skills of individual faculty members improved on an individual, as-needed basis through the Design Studio model.

To exemplify our faculty technology design studio activities, consider the following two examples. A group of three faculty members worked with teacher candidates to design and publish an electronic research journal focused on teaching activities within their partnership school. Each student was required to submit at least three manuscripts for the journal, while the teachers at the partnership site along with the university faculty members served as editors for the journal. The project required students to produce and edit electronic documents, and to communicate using various e-mail facilities. A group of four science education faculty explored opportunities for modeling hands-on science learning activities by assembling portable, "high-tech" laboratories that included electronic devices for collecting and analyzing data, such as sensing probes (light, temperature, motion, etc.), a seismograph, a telescope, and hand-held global positioning units. Faculty members designed hands-on learning activities that incorporated the portable science lab. The equipment was then used by students in our partnership classrooms as the faculty members modeled appropriate teaching methods with the devices.

The faculty members involved in this first-year experiences were well qualified and actively involved in the implementation of their design studio projects, which contributed to the overall success of our PT3 grant activities. However, there was some concern about widespread acceptance of design studio artifacts (plans and learning activities for specific courses) once we expanded participation to include all faculty members responsible for teacher preparation in the School of Education. Therefore, the PT3 project team took steps in year two of the grant to help ensure that all faculty members accepted and supported the goals and objectives of our PT3 grant. Each program area (e.g., Elementary Education, Special Education, etc.) was consulted individually, and challenged to identify ways in which technology-based learning activities could be infused into the teacher preparation curriculum. Given the positive experiences of the faculty technology design studio, it was expected that faculty acceptance and faculty participation would be high. Off-campus meetings were organized (with faculty being compensated for their time away from campus) to discuss ways that various learning activities produced during the design studios could be integrated into the curriculum. As a result of these meetings, program area faculty reached agreement on curricular alignment for the Illinois Core Technology Standards. That is to say, the faculty within each program area agreed upon which technology standards would be met in each required course. Further, faculty members agreed upon several assignments that would be required across multiple sections of required courses, regardless of instructor. These assignments would provide the teacher candidates with the opportunity to develop some type of technology integration plan or resource that could be used to demonstrate competency related to the various standards. It was also assumed that teacher candidates would include these artifacts in their electronic portfolios (more regarding electronic resources and portfolio tools is discussed later).

Partnership Technology Design Studios

Over the course of the grant, 16 partnership technology design studio sessions were organized for more than 700 SIUE teacher candidates and select mentor teachers from our partnership schools. Conducted by L.I.T.E.S.-trained teachers from the area, these sessions focused on discussion of effective technology integration strategies that promote engaged learning, examination of exemplary lesson and unit plans developed by L.I.T.E.S. teachers in the region, and collaboration in the design of learning activities for students. After designing teaching plans, each teacher candidate implemented his/her plan with students in the partnership school where they were assigned. Evaluative data regarding the effectiveness of the implementation were collected by the mentor teachers, discussed with the teacher candidates, and shared with university faculty and grant staff. Results indicated that these activities were very successful. Teacher candidates appreciated the opportunities to "practice" teaching with technology, and students in partnership schools were given learning opportunities that might not have occurred without the efforts supported by this grant. Our teacher candidates were excited about learning to use new technology and learning how to effectively integrate technology into their teaching. While the quality of projects varied from group to group and person to person, the majority of the teacher candidates came away from the field experience with several strong teaching plans that effectively integrated technology. The candidates shared their designs within their groups; therefore, while they only designed one unit, they ended the experience with several technology-integrated units in hand. As a whole, the teacher candidates felt these experiences prepared them to use technology when they entered the field after graduation.

Electronic Resources and Tools

To help us meet our third project objective, a corporate partner completed a two-year design process for a comprehensive suite of online content and tools that promote the development of electronic portfolios by SIUE teacher candidates. The system, called *TechReady*, was based on the Illinois Core Technology Standards (Illinois State Board of Education, 2003), and was designed to help students access learning resources, reflect on their learning, and demonstrate their teaching and technology competencies through the development of electronic portfolios. Ten faculty members, working with editorial staff from the corporate partner, developed content for the system during the Fall 2002 semester. The *TechReady* Web site provided students with the opportunity to take a self-assessment exam to measure their current technology competency. Further, the site assisted the students with developing a professional development plan to guide them through a process by which they could address the technology standards where their self-assessment indicated room for improvement. Finally, this site provided hands-on experiences to promote student understanding of issues related to integrating technology into teaching, including a "getting started" guide to introduce students to the most important issues related to each standard, and mini-projects to help students apply what they have learned. The system was implemented on a full scale in Spring 2003, after a year of prototype testing and revision (see http://www. siue.edu/education/TechReady/ to view the resource).

Integrating the *TechReady* resources into the teacher education programs proved more difficult than anticipated, despite the fact that members of the programs had helped to develop the content for the system. The unexpected problems were summed up in a comment made by one program director: "We're not ready to go with electronic portfolios, so I won't expect students to use that system." This statement directly contradicted information given to the designers of the *TechReady* system during their user-centered design interviews with faculty. However, given the power of this individual to sway faculty opinion, another tactic was developed.

After discussion with School of Education administrators, it was determined that the best approach may be to place the burden of meeting technology standards on the teacher candidates, rather than faculty and program areas. While some faculty members were not willing to directly teach any technology skills or components, they had agreed to require students to complete the technology-based assignments. This would make the teacher candidates responsible for collecting artifacts or evidence to demonstrate that they had met each of the standards. Faculty members would be responsible for grading individual assignments, but students would be responsible for collecting, compiling, and presenting these artifacts in a way that would illustrate their technology competencies.

Since this student-centered approach seemed to be acceptable to the major stakeholders, members of the grant team identified College LiveText (LiveText, Inc., 1997-2005) as the best option for our teacher candidates. Five faculty members were selected to attend LiveText training to learn about the electronic portfolio system from both a student and an instructor's perspective. These faculty members, in turn, trained a handful of faculty members from each program area to utilize LiveText in their courses. The final training of the remaining faculty was left to each department, assuring that each program area had someone who was knowledgeable about LiveText and could guide faculty through the system, explaining how to create, view, edit, and assess teacher candidate portfolios.

Following faculty training, the teacher candidates were introduced to the LiveText system with the expectation that faculty members would require some assignments to be submitted through LiveText, but would not be expected to directly teach students how to use it. Instead, introductory sessions were held for teacher candidates, and open lab times were established for them to "drop in" with specific LiveText questions. The teacher candidates were quick to utilize the LiveText portfolio tool, and just two months into the semester of adoption, students were logging in to LiveText, creating portfolios, and uploading artifacts to demonstrate technology competencies. While open lab hours with a LiveText expert were thought to be vital, it turned out to be unnecessary. A few teacher candidates came to open lab hours during the first few weeks to learn about LiveText, but ultimately they were happier working on their portfolios at home, or from the residence halls.

Evaluation of the TechReady online resource occurred in two ways. First, the process employed by the corporate partner to design and develop the system was highly dependent on the input of grant staff and faculty experts who contributed content for the system. Following interviews and surveys of students and faculty members, several iterations of a design document were completed before prototype development and testing occurred. This assured that the product would meet the expressed needs of faculty and students. Following implementation of the system, various types of quantitative data were collected using a Web-page statistics package. During the testing period, a total of 32,557 hits to the site were recorded. Visitors came from 803 different sites. Since there were only 564 unique users during the semester, this indicates that some users accessed *TechReady* from multiple sites (probably from home as well as at the university or a local school district). This result confirmed that our design goal of creating an anytime/anywhere learning resource accessible by students and faculty in various ways had been met. Analysis of the individual pages accessed by users indicated that content information about technology and technology integration was accessed much more frequently than information about portfolios, standards, and other resources.

LESSONS LEARNED

Our "ultimate" goal of producing graduates who can effectively integrate technology into their classrooms was measured in two ways. First, the percentage of our graduates who pass the state certification test, which includes items related to the state's technology standards, indicates the degree to which we are successful. As of this publication, 97% (1,109 out of 1,140) of our teacher candidates successfully passed the state's initial teacher certification test. Second, results from a survey of first-year teachers conducted by the State of Illinois compared our graduates with a state average of new teachers from other universities. Survey items pertinent to technology integration show that 30.6% (compared to a 57.4% state average) of our graduates who are new teachers felt that appropriate hardware and software was available for them to integrate technology into their classes, and 50% (compared to a 53.2% state average) felt well prepared to find ways to integrate technology into their classrooms. The results of the first item are likely related to the lack of availability of technology in the rural and high-risk urban districts surrounding SIUE. While the percentage for the second item seems low, we are at least gratified that we are comparable to other universities in the state. Certainly, further work on technology integration will help us improve these results.

Many things were learned by project staff and participants as part of the PT3 process, but two lessons stand out related to people and capabilities. We have found that the most important factor for our students to learn to effectively integrate technology was mentoring. Having accomplished teachers in the schools (L.I.T.E.S. mentors) who are demonstrating effective technology integration and advising our students during their attempts to design effective technology integration activities was invaluable. This stands in stark contrast to our assumption that university faculty need to provide effective models for technology integration. In many cases, the faculty members were not willing to do so, giving many different reasons as to why they couldn't or wouldn't address the technology standards and require technology-based assignments in their courses. In general, we heard the following reasons: (a) being uncomfortable with assigning a technology skill to students that the faculty members did not know how to do themselves, (b) being unfamiliar with the technology standards, or (c) not having enough time to teach the course content in addition to the technology standards. However, many interested and technology-competent faculty at the university had some positive influence as well. The incorporation of assignments and activities into the teacher education curriculum seemed to be more important than the ability of the faculty to "demonstrate" or model technology. Students helped each other as much as faculty helped students.

Finally, the other crucial factor that impacted our success was technology availability in the partnership school districts where our students complete their field experiences. We have many "bells and whistles" at the university with which to demonstrate best practices, but students soon realized the limitations of what was possible in the schools, and wanted simplified approaches for technology infrastructures that were not state-of-the-art. As schools in our region devote more resources toward technology, our success at preparing teachers to use technology will be greatly enhanced. Producing new teachers who are highly competent users of technology should provide impetus to schools to move more quickly to establish priorities for technology in local schools.

REFERENCES

Harel, I., & Papert, S. (Eds.). (1991). *Constructionism*. Norwood, NJ: Ablex.

Illinois State Board of Education. (2003). *Content area standards for educators*. Retrieved October 17, 2003, from http://www.isbe.net/profprep/standards.htm

Kahn, T. M., & Taber Ullah, L. N. (1998). *Learning by design: Integrating technology into the curriculum through student multimedia design projects*. Tucson, AZ: Zephyr Press.

Koehler, M. J., & Mishra, P. (2005). Teachers learning technology by design. *Journal of Computing in Teacher Education, 21*(3), 94-102.

LiveText, Inc. (1997-2005). *College LiveText* [Computer Program]. LaGrange, IL.

Nelson, W. A. (2003). Problem solving through design. In D. Knowlton & D. Sharp (Eds.), *New Directions for Teaching and Learning, 2003*, (95), 39-44. San Francisco: Jossey-Bass.

Nelson, W. A., Andris, J., & Keefe, D. (1991). Technology where they least expect it: A computer-intensive teacher education curriculum. *Computers in the Schools*, 8(1/2/3), 103-109.

Orey, M., Rieber, L., King, J., & Matzko, M. (2000, April). *The Studio: Curriculum reform in an instructional technology graduate program*. Paper presented at the annual meeting of the American Educational Research Association, New Orleans, LA.

Perkins, D. N. (1986). *Knowledge as design*. Hillsdale, NJ: Lawrence Erlbaum.

Rieber, L. P. (2000). The studio experience: Educational reform in instructional technology. In D. G. Brown (Ed.), *Best practices in computer enhanced teaching and learning* (pp. 195-196). Winston-Salem, NC: Wake Forest Press.

doi:10.1300/J025v23n03_06

Valeria Amburgey

One Model of Professional Development for Higher Education Faculty

SUMMARY. Northern Kentucky University's College of Education's faculty realizes that the infusion of technology into the teacher education program is important. Support for the infusion of technology was evident when the faculty adopted the ISTE *Recommended Foundations for Teachers* and a five-year technology plan in 1998. Interviews with the faculty during the 1999-2000 academic year identified three primary barriers for infusion of technology into the curriculum: (a) access to technology, (b) training on how to use the technology, and (c) time to re-design curriculum. If increased access to technology is provided to higher education faculty, how should the training and time issues be addressed? doi:10.1300/J025v23n03_07 *[Article copies available for a fee from The Haworth Document Delivery Service: 1-800-HAWORTH. E-mail address: <docdelivery@haworthpress.com> Website: <http://www.HaworthPress.com> © 2006 by The Haworth Press, Inc. All rights reserved.]*

VALERIA AMBURGEY is Professor of Mathematics and Technology Education and Coordinator for Technology, TLT Project Director, Northern Kentucky University, College of Education and Human Services, BEP 272, Highland Heights, KY 41099 (E-mail: amburgey@nku.edu).
This project is supported by a PT3 grant from the United States Department of Education.

[Haworth co-indexing entry note]: "One Model of Professional Development for Higher Education Faculty." Amburgey, Valeria. Co-published simultaneously in *Computers in the Schools* (The Haworth Press, Inc.) Vol. 23, No. 3/4, 2006, pp. 105-113; and: *Teaching Teachers to Use Technology* (ed: D. LaMont Johnson, and Kulwadee Kongrith) The Haworth Press, Inc., 2006, pp. 105-113. Single or multiple copies of this article are available for a fee from The Haworth Document Delivery Service [1-800-HAWORTH, 9:00 a.m. - 5:00 p.m. (EST). E-mail address: docdelivery@haworthpress.com].

KEYWORDS. Model of Professional Development, professional development, higher education faculty, Northern Kentucky University

The preparation of teachers to meet the challenges of current school and classroom environments is the primary concern of most schools and/or colleges of education. The needs of society often determine the educational needs of students. Technology is a primary problem-solving tool in many aspects of society today and has become more important in the educational environment. Future teachers need to be trained not only on how to use the technology but also on the appropriate instructional applications of technology in a learning environment.

Robinson (2000) stated that changes in the use of technology in the classroom necessitate strategic planning and forethought. He emphasized the importance in the planning and preparation of the institution's most valuable asset-people. Hixson and Tinzmann (1990) described institutional change as both a people and a policy process. They noted that professional development is the primary vehicle through which important educational changes are implemented as one of four overriding principles.

Northern Kentucky University's (NKU) College of Education faculty recognized the importance of preparing teachers to be technology proficient when they adopted the ISTE *Recommended Foundations for Teachers* in 1998. The Technology Committee for the College of Education made the recommendation to adopt these standards as part of the continuous review and assessment of our teacher education program. Along with the recommendations for the technology standards, the Technology Committee recommended a technology plan for the College of Education that outlined four broad goals over the next five years: (a) to provide the students and faculty in the College of Education with the most advanced multimedia teaching and learning environments, (b) to assist faculty in becoming fully competent in using multimedia in their teaching, (c) to develop a plan for maintenance and regular software and hardware upgrades of the faculty and staff computers within the College of Education, and (d) to revise the manner in which the College of Education ensures and verifies that undergraduate and graduate students completing a degree or certification program at NKU have the necessary skills in using technology in the classroom.

Although the College of Education faculty was supportive of the technology standards and the technology plan, there did exist some barriers to the fulfillment of our goals. During the 1999-2000 academic year, an independent researcher interviewed the faculty and identified three primary barriers to the infusion of technology within our teacher education program: (a) access to technology, (b) training on how to use the technology, and (c) time to redesign curriculum. Two of the goals from the technology plan addressed the access to technology and the training of the faculty. The question remained how to address the needs of the faculty in order to infuse technology within our teacher education program.

COMMUNITY FACTORS

Northern Kentucky University's faculty are very active and aware of statewide initiatives. The College of Education continually reviews their teacher education program for many reasons, including assuring that state education initiatives are assimilated into the program. The state of Kentucky placed importance on the use of technology within the classroom with the implementation of the Kentucky Education Technology System (KETS) during the early 1990s. In May 1999, the Education Professional Standards Board implemented a new technology standard for both new and experienced teachers. The statewide standard is based upon the ISTE technology standards for teachers. Kentucky teachers are expected to use technology to support instruction; access and manipulate data; enhance professional growth and productivity; communicate and collaborate with colleagues, parents, and the community; and conduct research.

Several reports have noted that many teachers, while aware of the need for technology infusion in the curriculum, do not feel prepared to use technology effectively. In January 1999, a report from the Kentucky Institute for Education Research (KIER) noted that 26% of all new teachers in the state of Kentucky felt moderately/very poorly prepared to "use technology as an integral part of instruction." Northern Kentucky University conducted a survey of principals in the area in 1999 and found that 25% of them felt that their teachers were moderately/very poorly prepared. The Northern Kentucky Cooperative for Education Services (NKCES, 1999) noted in their *Professional Development Needs Assessment* that 12 out of 25 priority needs of area educators involved one or more areas of technology.

These reports supported NKU's College of Education initiatives to infuse technology into their teacher education program. Some faculty had already started to include technology standards in their curriculum.

The question still remained regarding the obstacles to overcome in fully implementing the technology standards and the technology plan. Professional development of the faculty was a critical component in these initiatives.

NKU'S TLT MODEL

NKU's College of Education was fortunate to receive funding from the U. S. Department of Education as part of their Preparing Tomorrow's Teachers to Use Technology (PT3) initiatives. A capacity building grant during the 1999-2000 year and an ongoing implementation grant have provided us with the means to implement the initiatives identified in our technology plan. Within our Teaching, Learning and Technology (TLT) Project, we identified three main goals: (a) creating technology-rich environments, (b) faculty professional development, and (c) student professional development. These three goals addressed three of the four goals within our technology plan. TLT Project Goal 1 addresses the access to technology barrier, and TLT Project Goal 3 addresses the curricular review and redesign issues. TLT Project Goal 2 addresses both the training and time for faculty to learn about technology and to apply their new knowledge and skills to their coursework.

As part of the TLT grant activities, a maximum of five faculty received a one course (three semester hours) reduction in their teaching load each semester in order to participate in formal technology training. Faculty who had the option of receiving this reassigned time had teaching responsibilities in the teacher education program. This includes faculty from the College of Arts and Sciences as well as the College of Education.

The technology coordinator for the College of Education met with the faculty with reassigned time at the beginning of each semester. Each faculty provided the technology coordinator with a list of his/her personal goals for technology training. The technology coordinator and the faculty member subsequently set up a schedule for meeting formally throughout the semester for their professional development. If applicable, samples of course syllabi, assignments, or other course material were collected at the beginning of the semester.

The list of personal goals for each faculty member became the individual professional growth plan for the semester. Topics, which were most representative of the types of goals requested by the faculty, included learning how to turn a computer on, use of personal productivity tools (i.e., word processing, spreadsheets, databases), and the use of the Internet in instructional activities. Developing of professional Web pages or providing for enhancement of courses through the use of the Web were frequent requests for training.

During each of the formal technology training sessions with the faculty, the technology coordinator designed "lessons" around the faculty's personal goals. The formal training included lectures or demonstrations of instructional activities incorporating technology as well as hands-on experiences with specific technology. Some faculty needs included knowledge and skills that are better served by colleagues within other departments on campus. For example, a chemistry professor was invited to work with the math and science education faculty on using of computer based laboratories (CBLs).

Some faculty were very comfortable with technology while other faculty were "tentative" in their technology abilities. Formal professional development sessions were designed for all reassigned faculty in one group as well as on an individual basis. One faculty member, as an example, was so new to technology that he/she did not feel comfortable with turning on the computer or using e-mail. The technology coordinator met once a week with this faculty member and provided individualized instruction on basic computer use.

A non-credit class was set up on Blackboard for faculty to experience a Web-enhanced course. Examples of course documents and discussion forums were included on this Web site to demonstrate another method of sharing course information with students. Faculty were encouraged to interact with Blackboard in order to experience the student's perspective.

The technology coordinator conducted periodic checks to see if the personal goals of the faculty were being met. During the middle of the semester, faculty were asked to re-evaluate their personal goals, because needs may have changed based upon training already received or the redesigning of course material. This midterm check allowed the faculty to reflect on their original goals and for everyone to evaluate their accomplishments. Future formal training sessions were redesigned based upon these reflections. A final reflection was completed at the end of the semester: Did the training they experienced provide them with the necessary knowledge and skills to assist with the infusion of technology into the courses they teach? What are the final results? Copies of revised syllabi, instructional activities, and Web pages were often artifacts that represented the impact of their formal training.

Informal Professional Development

Reassigned time for formal professional development training was provided to a maximum of five faculty members each semester. Other faculty were in various stages of technology proficiency. Even those who previously participated in the formal professional development needed additional training due to the ever-changing field of technology.

Technology seminars were regularly scheduled to provide opportunities for both faculty and students within the teacher education program to learn new technologies or explore beyond the basics of specific technology skills. Seminars were conducted by NKU students, faculty, or area educators. It was not unusual to have faculty who received reassigned time for professional development in previous semesters to conduct one or more of these seminars to share with others what they were doing in their courses. Area educators provided updates on statewide initiatives or shared projects from their schools or districts.

Outcomes

To date, there have been 23 teacher education faculty who have participated in the formal technology professional development. This includes faculty from across the university who are involved in the teacher education program. The faculty represents every level of certification (i.e., elementary, middle, secondary, special education, etc.) and demonstrates the collaboration between the College of Arts and Sciences and the College of Education.

Statements from the faculty who participated in the training indicate that the training was valuable for them and the reassigned time allowed them to practice what they learned while redesigning course curriculum. As an example, a quote from one of the special education faculty members noted his experiences with Web page development:

> Technology training experiences have provided me with the time and resources needed to learn about, design and develop a personal/professional web page. This page provides my students with www access to class syllabi and materials that are related to the courses I teach. I have also created links that serve as a portal for my students to access course related information from the www that I have screened for accuracy and quality. This page keeps expanding as I develop more skills and discover additional ways to use the internet as one of my teaching tools.

This same faculty member further explained how he designs and implements instructional activities that incorporate the use of the Internet:

> Prior to this training, I seldom used the Internet as a classroom resource. Now, it has become a part of my preparation for many lessons and activities. Students that want to know more than what is provided in class can use the URL's that I provide as a means of enriching their learning experiences. In many classes, I ask my students to gather information from sources on the www then read and be prepared to discuss this material in class. I find that they like discovering these new sources of information and prefer accessing information from the www over traditional library research. The technology training has enabled me to lead my students in these activities.

Incorporating the Internet into the teacher education program was a common theme among faculty. Some faculty, developed their own Web pages and utilized these as additional resources for their students. The quote from a math educator points out another method of utilizing Web-based resources:

> This semester, I am using aspects of Blackboard.com such as posting my syllabus and assignments and posting grades. Students really like accessing their grades without having to wait for me to return papers in class. It also cuts down on the phone calls from students when they can either find information on the web or email their questions to me.

The use of Blackboard has increased significantly since the first round of professional development for faculty began. All colleges and departments have one or more courses now available as a Web-based or Web-enhanced class. Blackboard provides a relatively user-friendly means for faculty to provide information to their students via the Web while also providing some level of security for course-related information. For many faculty, the ease of posting information for their students in Blackboard outweighs the sometimes negative aspect of having all courses look alike using the course template format.

The professional development appears to have increased the confidence level of the faculty in utilizing technology in their classes. As noted by one of the science education faculty: "I am now able to require much more use of technology from the students as I learn to use it more myself."

As part of the TLT project, classrooms are also being upgraded to include increased access to technology for faculty and students. One of the faculty members who participated in the reassigned time and formal professional training had the opportunity to teach in one of the newly renovated classrooms before retiring.

This classroom includes an instructor's station that has a computer, VCR, and document camera connected to a ceiling-mounted projection system and controlled by a wall-mounted smart panel. The back of the classroom has computer stations with large monitors to provide opportunities for cooperative group activities. He noted that the technology training was very personally beneficial and also that "classrooms without this equipment should be put on the "soon to be abolished" list! If we are going to practice what we preach about constructivist teaching, then we must have the facilities to do so."

CONCLUSION

NKU's College of Education recently reviewed the National Educational Technology Standards (NETS) for students and teachers. The state technology standards are a close match to the new NETS standards. The faculty have formally adopted the NETS for Teachers standards to replace the ISTE recommended foundations used in 1998.

NKU's TLT model for faculty professional development appears to be successful. The comments from the faculty who have participated in the formal training and received the reassigned time indicate their increased level of confidence and new ideas for using technology in their coursework. Even the faculty member who needed the individualized training has made the transition to using technology in the middle grades language arts methods classes by implementing a system of e-mail pen pals between area middle school students and the middle grades language arts teacher education candidates.

Teachers, regardless of grade level or content expertise, often tend to teach the way they were taught. Future teachers will not consider using new instructional strategies or technology unless exposed to those strategies and skills somewhere in their training. NKU's teacher education faculty are now modeling appropriate and effective uses of technology within the instructional environment. It is doubtful that they would be doing this without the time and training provided through the TLT grant activities.

The major challenge now will be how to allow faculty the opportunity to continue to develop in their knowledge and skills with technology. The university is in the planning stages of establishing two centers that will provide training and support for the entire campus community. The Instructional Technology Development Center and the Faculty Development Center are fully functioning since spring 2002 and will go a long way in sustaining the College of Education's faculty needs.

REFERENCES

Forward Quest Task Force. (1999, March 24). *The future of public schools business focus group.* Covington, KY: Forward Quest.

Hixson, J & Tinzmann, M.B. (1990). *What changes are generating new needs for professional development?* Retrieved April 25, 2006 from http://www.ncrel.org/sdrs/areas/rpl_esys/profdev.htm

International Society for Technology in Education (1998). *ISTE recommended foundations in technology for all teachers.* Retrieved April 25, 2006 from http://www.iste.org/Standards/index.html

International Society for Technology in Education (2000). *National educational technology standards (NETS) for teachers project.* Retrieved April 25, 2006 from http://cnets.iste.org/index3.html

Kentucky Department of Education. *New teacher standards for preparation and certification.* Retrieved April 25, 2006 from http://www.kde.state.ky.us/otec/epsb/standards/new_teach_stds.asp

Kentucky Institute for Education Research (1999). *The preparation of teachers for Kentucky schools: A longitudinal study of new teachers* (Summary Report for Years 1996-1990). Frankfort, KY.

Northern Central Regional Educational Laboratory. *Critical Issue: Providing professional development for effective technology use.* Retrieved April 25, 2006 from http://www.ncrel.org/sdrs/areas/issues/methods/technlgy/te1000.htm

Northern Kentucky Cooperative for Education Services (April 1999). *Region wide top 25 priority needs.* Highland Heights, KY.

Robinson, E.T. (2000). Strategic planning for technological change. The human component. *Syllabus, 14*(4), 54-55, 65.

doi:10.1300/J025v23n03_07

Inquiry Learning and Technology: A Model for Teacher Education Programs

SUMMARY. PT3 implementation grant funds have been used to restructure a teacher education program to meet the National Educational Technology Standards (NETS) defined by the International Society for Technology in Education (ISTE). The Brigham Young University PT3 implementation grant supported design teams of teacher education and content area faculty who enriched pre-service teacher education courses and K-12 curricula with inquiry-based technology integration. The teams modeled technology-enhanced instruction to pre-service teachers who then wrote similar lesson plans that they implemented during K-12 field experiences. Technology-enhanced unit plans written by pre-service teachers were coded to see which NETS were met. A correlation study was done to compare the innovation of the lessons and the NETS standards. The results of this study indicate that, when inquiry-based instruction is a focus of technology integration, learning is collaborative, student-centered, and develops critical thinking skills in students. doi:10.1300/J025v23n03_08 *[Article copies available for a fee from The Haworth Document Delivery Service: 1-800-HAWORTH. E-mail address: <docdelivery@haworthpress.com> Website: <http://www.HaworthPress.com> © 2006 by The Haworth Press, Inc. All rights reserved.]*

NANCY WENTWORTH is Professor and Associate Chair, Department of Teacher Education, McKay School of Education, Brigham Young University, Provo, UT 84602 (E-mail: nancy_wentworth@byu.edu).

[Haworth co-indexing entry note]: "Inquiry Learning and Technology: A Model for Teacher Education Programs." Wentworth, Nancy. Co-published simultaneously in *Computers in the Schools* (The Haworth Press, Inc.) Vol. 23, No. 3/4, 2006, pp. 115-129; and: *Teaching Teachers to Use Technology* (ed: D. LaMont Johnson, and Kulwadee Kongrith) The Haworth Press, Inc., 2006, pp. 115-129. Single or multiple copies of this article are available for a fee from The Haworth Document Delivery Service [1-800-HAWORTH, 9:00 a.m. - 5:00 p.m. (EST). E-mail address: docdelivery@haworthpress.com].

Available online at http://cits.haworthpress.com
doi:10.1300/J025v23n03_08

KEYWORDS. Technology integration, inquiry learning, action research, collaboration, teacher education, technology standards

INTRODUCTION

The federal Preparing Tomorrow's Teachers to Use Technology (PT3) grants supported the development of models for integrating technology into teacher education programs and K-12 curriculum. In many early models of implementing technology into teacher education programs, prospective teachers took a computer literacy class separate from content methods classes and rarely engaged in real collaboration on how teachers could integrate technology into authentic learning experiences (Kearsley, 1998). By focusing merely on how to use computers, technology training failed by not addressing how to teach students more effectively using a variety of technological tools. Programs often emphasized "how to use specific types of technology [rather than] how to solve educational problems using technology when needed and appropriate" (p. 50). Josten's Learning Corporation and the American Association of School Administrators reported that teacher training in technology, while readily available, focused merely on basic computer operation (Jostens, 1997). Many public school classrooms have not linked instruction to real-life situations or technology integration so the field experiences of pre-service teachers have been limited (Pappillion & Cellitti, 1996). These studies suggest that teachers need to learn how to integrate technology into instruction so that content can be taught more meaningfully and effectively. Technology integration should cause teachers to develop different perspectives through the rethinking of teaching and learning (Riedl, 1995; Ritchie & Wilburg, 1994). Teaching with technology causes teachers to confront their established beliefs about instruction and their traditional roles as classroom teachers.

The PT3-funded restructuring efforts at Brigham Young University (BYU) were designed to alleviate these weaknesses in traditional teacher preparation through simultaneous redesign of teacher preparation and K-12 curricula, enriching *both* through technology integration. Preparing tomorrow's teachers to integrate technology into their instruction requires university faculty to provide pre-service teachers with examples of and experiences with learning enhanced by technology. For this to occur, teacher educators must first adopt the knowledge, dispositions, and practices associated with effective technology integration. Successfully integrating technology into a teacher preparation program includes, at a minimum, rethinking curriculum and methods of instruction, providing mentoring and support for associated faculty members, and developing collaborative relationships among university faculty, pre-service teachers, teachers, and school districts.

This paper will describe the BYU inquiry-based model that implemented strategies for technology integration by creating curriculum design teams composed of university faculty, public school personnel, and instructional design and technology specialists. Design teams developed instructional activities that implemented technology through inquiry learning as a way to model appropriate uses. Then the teacher education instructors assigned their students to develop similar K-12 technology-enhanced lessons.

BRIGHAM YOUNG UNIVERSITY INQUIRY-BASED MODEL

BYU graduates over 1,000 teachers each year. The teacher education program currently provides lab access to modern technologies for students and requires pre-service teachers to take one instructional technology course. Prior to the grant there was support for faculty who self-selected to use technology in undergraduate courses, but there was not a systematic effort to integrate technology into the overall curriculum.

Based on this history and the perceived need to move BYU along in the effective use of technology, a concerted effort was made to mentor faculty and build alignment around issues of technology integration. These goals were achieved through three major project activities: (a) creating curriculum design teams composed of university faculty (including teacher education and content-specific methods instructors) and public school personnel, (b) holding yearly summer institutes and other training and collaboration opportunities that focus on the infusion of technology, and (c) facilitating alignment among BYU activities, partner districts, the state office of education, and other teacher preparation programs in the state.

In addition to these activities, informal lunch-time meetings provided venues for faculty to share their use of technology and allowed for just-in-time technical and instructional support to help the design teams as they learned to integrate technology. The yearly grant activities provided a framework for the participation of three specific design teams: Elementary Science and Mathematics, Inquiry Learning, and Action Research.

GRANT ACTIVITIES

Year One: Development of Design Teams

During the first academic year the grant focused on developing curriculum design teams. BYU teacher education faculty and public school colleagues attended several day-long workshops focused on the integration of technology into K-12 curriculum and the development of the skills needed to use technology in instruction. Experts from Apple Computers, INTEL Teach to the Future, Casio, and the Utah Education Network were among the workshop facilitators. Members of the PT3 leadership team introduced the ISTE National Education Technology Standards (NETS) and met with participants to discuss what they valued in their courses and how technology might enhance what they do. Design teams began to form as participants with common goals met at workshops focused on helping faculty integrate technology into their instruction.

Midway through the year the PT3 leadership team asked participants to organize themselves into specific design teams. In the first year of the grant eight design teams signed contracts outlining their goals. Each contract was unique in the support that would be offered and the goals that would be met, but the teams did share some activities. The teams agreed to attend additional workshops, meet regularly as a group, and attend a summer institute. The teams received funds to attend some of these activities, but only when they could show lesson plans, research presentations or papers, or student products resulting from PT3 participation. Members of three design teams presented their work at a national technology conference, Society for Information Technology and Teacher Education (SITE), during the first year of the grant.

A summer institute culminating the first year focused on two goals: electronic portfolio development and technology integration into the curriculum, with examples from public school classrooms. Design teams met with other teams to discuss their uses of technology. They also met with the external evaluators for interviews about their work.

Year Two:
Developing Technology-Enhanced Teacher
Education Curriculum

The most obvious change in PT3 activities the second year was the move away from outside presenters at workshops to presentations by design teams at monthly brown bag meetings. Teams shared ways in which they were integrating technology into their teacher education courses and presented student products. Pre-service teachers at BYU were creating educational portfolios and inquiry-based, technology-enhanced K-12 curriculum. Four faculty members attended an INTEL Teach to the Future workshop and were using the program in one elementary and two secondary education courses. As these products were developed, design teams began to create rubrics for evaluating the products based on the ISTE standards. At PT3 brown bags several design teams presented the lessons and rubrics they had developed.

A unique activity during the second year was an excursion by many design team members to the Classroom Connect Conference in Las Vegas. This excursion was organized and funded by the PT3 leadership team and designed to bring teacher education faculty, district personnel, and mentor teachers together to discuss technology, teacher education, and K-12 curriculum. Design team members decided on sessions to attend as teams prior to the conference. The external evaluators wrote, "Not only did this event have the single greatest impact on faculty's perceptions, but also served as a powerful example of the serendipitous use of grant resources. This is clearly an excellent example of creative use of resources to promote long-term technology goals. . . . [T]his activity allowed for very important bonding to take place and enabled much of the superb work that has followed" (Connell & Johnson, 2002, p. 10).

Another new activity for design team members during the second year of the grant was to take the Instructional Psychology and Technology (IP&T 286) course designed for pre-service teacher education candidates. Participating in this course helped faculty become more aware of the kinds of technologies they could expect students to use in their course assignments. Participants mentioned that taking this course helped them find ways to better integrate those skills into their courses and research. Thirty-five faculty members went through the IP&T 286 course. One faculty member said: "The course was a great opportunity to learn some technology skills that I don't think I would have learned on my own." Some stated that the technology course was outdated and needed to focus less on skills acquisition, though important, and more on good instructional design and the seamless integration of technology into instruction and lesson plan preparation. Because of this feedback the course has since been redesigned to better model the integration of technology into instruction. Inquiry-based instruction became the basis for examples of technology-enhanced lessons.

Another opportunity provided by the grant was to attend the annual SITE conference. Twenty-three people attended this conference (including faculty, clinical faculty, staff, dean, and assistant to the dean). The external evaluators stated that the strong presence of BYU's faculty at this conference did a great deal to advance BYU's reputation as a leader in the field of information technology in teacher education. Not only did attending this conference allow for exposure of the 23 attendees to national ideas and trends, but motivated faculty to publish and present their research findings at an international forum as well. In the minds of many faculty this served to legitimize their work. As one faculty member put it, "The grant provided an opportunity for me to participate in SITE, which was a wonderful experience. This allowed me to collaborate with different people and broadened my professional horizons." Another said, "With support from the PT3 grant and the University to attend national and international conferences, we have learned from users of educational technology far and wide. It is during presentations and interactions at these conferences that we have experienced our major 'aha' insights-moments when we have caught glimpses of the potential of technology as a transforming influence in our teacher preparation program. We have returned to BYU after each conference more committed than ever to help our students enter the schools prepared for the roles they are expected to assume as technologically capable classroom teachers."

The summer institute at the end of the second year introduced participants to WebQuests, a learning model for integrating Internet research into inquiry-based learning, and an effective way to help both faculty and pre-service teachers integrate technology into instruction. WebQuests help students navigate the Internet with a clear task in mind, retrieve data from multiple resources, and increase critical-thinking skills (Dodge, 1998). Raizen, Sellwood, Todd, and Vickers (1995) found WebQuest activities to be useful tools for enhancing the development of transferable skills that help students bridge the gap between schools and "real world" experiences. Dede (1998) found that using WebQuests resulted in at least four kinds of improvements in educational outcomes: (a) Guided inquiry, project-based collaboration and mentoring relationships have increased learner motivation, (b) technology-based instruction enabled students to learn-how-to-learn and master advanced topics, (c) students in team environments performed complex tasks and created intricate products by acting as experts, and (d) as teachers mastered these new models of learning, students achieved better outcomes on standardized tests.

We encouraged design team members to invite public school teachers to a three-day workshop where they would work together to develop K-12 curriculum using WebQuests. They also created assignments for teacher education courses that would not only address course content but also require the pre-service teachers to develop WebQuest K-12 lessons for their field experiences. The members of the Inquiry Learning Design Team said in an interview, "The format of this workshop allowed us to not only learn basic skills, but to actually create a WebQuest. We also received feedback from other teams regarding how it could be improved; and, following the workshop, we met frequently to implement these suggestions. Later, we would develop three more WebQuests for inclusion in our course." The external evaluators reported that the 2002 summer institute, with its emphasis on WebQuests, was very positively received by faculty. This fact was brought forcefully home by one faculty member who said, "I think it's important during each institute that you actually are required to create a project while you are there. Otherwise things taper off and we never reach closure on anything."

Year Three: Moving Toward Sustainability

The third year of the grant saw the expansion of many of the design teams. The original eight teams had grown to fifteen. Some teams remained intact. Others split into more than one team as new members began to participate. The design teams began to work more deliberately with state and district specialists and classroom teachers. They focused their activities on embedding technology permanently into teacher education courses with demonstrations, assignments, and accountability. Some teams began to expect technology lessons and activities from their students as they moved into a public school experience. Design team members joined statewide initiatives to link technology efforts in pre-service programs with mentoring and evaluation programs during the first and second year of teaching. The brown bags continued every month and a "Techie Talk" was added to teach the skills demonstrated during the brown bags. Twenty-four (24) design team members attended the SITE technology conference and presented 15 papers on the integration of technology into the BYU teacher education program.

The final summer institute featured Levels of Technology Integration (LoTI) (k12.albemarle.org/MurrayElem/principal/doe99/ techuse.html). Participants evaluated the level of technology integration in their teacher education courses. They reported that this activity helped them understand how lessons enhanced with Internet research and problem solving supported high-level thinking more than lessons that were enhanced with technology production only.

DESIGN TEAMS AT WORK

Elementary Science and Mathematics Design Team

Marv and Eula formed a design team based on the desire to integrate technology into their elementary education science and mathematics methods courses. Both were "mature" faculty members who had spent the majority of their teaching career using "typewriters and ditto machine" technology. They felt they were faced with a steep learning curve that required them to "increase our fluency and flexibility with technology, transform our methods courses to include technology activities, and increase the use of technology by our pre-service teachers." Each observed their students using technology effectively in their portfolios. The PT3 workshops and the summer institute provided them with examples of ways to model technology to their students. For them, the initial year of the PT3 grant was a time to discover software, Web sites, and tools that could enhance instruction. By the end of the year they wanted to learn how to integrate these newly discovered technology tools into the methods curriculum.

Eula attended the SITE conference in the spring of the first year and began to understand how she could move her lesson development to an inquiry model and ask her students to do the same. Both she and Marv were influenced by the summer institute presentations by public school teachers who were using inquiry learning in their instruction. Eula and Marv began to develop lessons for their courses that would model inquiry learning. They rewrote assignments asking their students to write K-12 lessons that followed the models they had used in their courses. Eula expressed a desire to present at the SITE conference the following year, discussing her personal growth with technology integration, and began year two with the research of her own practice with technology in mind.

Inquiry Learning Design Team

In October 2001 Roni Jo, a secondary literacy specialist, Leigh, an elementary science specialist, and Brenda, an elementary literacy specialist attended the Classroom Connect Conference. As a result they began to see themselves as a design team that would focus on inquiry-based learning. They signed a PT3 contract agreeing to attend brown bags, to write a technology assignment for their students, to attend the WebQuest workshop, and to participate in grant-related evaluation. Because of the time they had spent together at the Classroom Connect Conference and subsequent discussions, they felt that WebQuests were an ideal strategy to combine their interests in inquiry-based learning and technology integration. Leigh used a WebQuest to introduce her course in which she focused on issues related to teaching science. She had pre-service candidates construct WebQuests for K-6 students. Students were able to discuss the use of the Internet in their teaching and how to find and integrate scientifically and educationally appropriate Web sites. For her literacy methods course, Brenda developed a problem-based learning WebQuest that helped students explore the meaning of balanced literacy in grades K-6. When students went out to the field, they created WebQuests to give to their peers based on questions that arose from their field experience. Students reported that the WebQuest was their greatest accomplishment thus far in their teacher education program. The third member of the team, Roni Jo, helped them address the ways WebQuests were used to cover the content of the course, and how WebQuests supported subject area standards and technology standards. Roni Jo reported that modeling WebQuests to teach content helped students design WebQuests for the K-12 classroom.

The design team felt that one of the most valuable things they taught their students was how to select and integrate age-appropriate material from the Web into their classroom. "The use of WebQuests in our methods courses was useful to help students gain skills for teaching elementary science and literature. WebQuests supported technology integration in ways that model how they might integrate technology into their classroom." They all mentioned that their students were becoming more critical consumers of information. Additionally, they felt that technology worked best when it was used to "construct" rather than as a medium for delivery or presentation, especially, when inquiry learning is the main goal. They also commented that their students felt WebQuests were a more personal way of learning the material and allowed for more personal expression.

Action Research Design Team

Two faculty members in secondary education had worked together for six years as co-facilitators of a cohort of students. Nancy, secondary mathematics education specialist, and Merrell, secondary history specialist, began as a design team in the first year of the grant. They had participated in the workshops and the SITE conference. They attended an INTEL Teach to the Future program and began to include technology assignments in both the cohort projects and other teacher education courses. Most of the early students' curriculum projects focused on the use of the Internet and PowerPoint to plan and present their work. The PT3 workshops helped Nancy and Merrell include reflection in the projects as well as technology.

During the second and third year of the grant they rewrote an assignment for their cohort students stressing technology as an integral component. They asked cohort students working in the same schools to team up to prepare an action research project. The students had to select an educational issue that impacted learning in their school; research the issue on the Internet; collect data from students, faculty, administrators, and parents; use spreadsheet programs to analyze their data; and prepare a PowerPoint presentation on the issue. They had to take a stand on the issue and suggest actions that would address the issue in the school.

Merrell said, "We wanted to ensure that technology was used to acquire and organize the students' projects and to present these in a more professional and scholarly way. . . . This was one assignment that required a pragmatic use of skills, knowledge, and dispositions associated with technology." Their experience with these programs gave the pre-service teachers confidence to ask their students to do similar projects.

INQUIRY LEARNING AND THE NATIONAL EDUCATIONAL TECHNOLOGY STANDARDS

Eighty-three inquiry-based units created by pre-service teachers were coded by three faculty members working with PT3 grant support and evaluated them using the rubric in Table 1. The rubric was developed to establish correlations between ISTE standards met and the type of instruction used. The first four items on the rubric come from Carroll's (2000) definition of instructional practices using technology that has the potential of creating new learning environments in the classroom: (a) student-centered not teacher-centered, (b) collaborative work not isolated work, (c) active learning not passive learning, and (d) instruction in critical thinking not factual/literal thinking. Lessons were coded on a scale from 0 to 3 based on how much the lessons moved from traditional instruction to more innovative instruction. The last six items relate to the extent that the unit plan meets each of the six ISTE standards for students: (a) basic operations and concepts; (b) social, ethical, and human issues; (c) technology productivity tools; (d) technology

TABLE 1. Intercorrelations Between Instructional Practices and ISTE Standards for Students

Instructional Practices	1	2	3	4	5	6	7	8	9	10
1. Teacher centered–student centered	—	0.65	0.78	0.57	−0.14	0.05	0.41	−0.60	0.52	0.53
2. Isolated–collaborative		—	0.69	0.42	−0.17	0.13	0.52	−0.22	0.65	0.55
3. Passive–active			—	0.65	−0.15	0.16	0.45	−0.20	0.69	0.65
4. Factual/literal–problem-solving				—	−0.07	0.22	0.26	0.01	0.51	0.83
ISTE Standards										
5. Operation					—	−0.04	0.12	−0.03	−0.21	−0.11
6. Social issues						—	0.19	0.02	0.00	0.20
7. Productivity tools							—	−0.16	0.21	0.29
8. Communication tools								—	−0.07	−0.06
9. Research tools									—	0.63
10. Problem-solving tools										—

communications tools; (e) technology research tools; and (f) technology problem solving and decision making. Each standard received a score of 0 if the standard was not present in the lesson, 1 if the standard was present but not central to the lesson, 2 if the standard was present and central to the lesson, and 3 if the standard was present, central to the lesson, and enhanced the learning in the lesson. The results of these evaluations provide insight into the relationship between instructional practices and the ISTE standards. A correlation analysis was done to compare instructional practices and the ISTE standard met. The complete correlation is found in Table 1.

The instructional practice correlations are all significant except the two between "teacher centered-student centered" and "isolated-collaborative" with "factual/literal thinking-problem solving" comparison. This result supports Carroll's claim that these instructional practices are similar in their reflection of innovation when they are used to create new learning environments. The correlations between the ISTE standards are all low (except between "research" and "problem solving"). This supports the distinct nature of these standards. The correlations between the instructional practices and the ISTE standards are of most interest in this study. They are the correlations in the shaded box in Table 1.

The significant correlations are between the instructional practice of "collaborative learning" and "active learning" and "research" and "problem solving" standards and between the instructional practice of "problem solving" and the "problem solving" standard. The ISTE standards of "research," "problem solving," and "productivity" have high (but not significant) correlations with all of the instructional practices. This seems to indicate that, when the unit plan supports the standards of research and problem solving, it helps to create the innovative learning environment described by Carroll (2000). The correlations between the standards or "operations" and "communications" and the instructional practices are almost all negative (but not highly significant). This indicates that, when a unit plan supports learning the operations of computers or supports communications with computers, the unit does not necessarily support the innovative learning environment described by Carroll (2000). The "social issues" standard has neither negative nor high correlations with the learning practices, probably because so few of the lessons were coded as meeting this standard.

CONCLUSION

The BYU PT3 grant provided workshops, summer institutes, and research opportunities that encouraged design teams to model appropriate uses of technology in inquiry-based instruction. Faculty perceptions of instructional technology progressed from being viewed as complex and too time consuming to being viewed as a natural part of instruction. In the words of one faculty member: "I see technology as more simplified now. For me it went from being an external thing to a tool that can enhance teaching and learning." The central role of technology was reflected in many of the interviews where it was described as "a resource to supplement and improve what we do." Three themes emerge from the PT3 activities: (a) Curriculum design teams were organized according to naturally occurring alliances in the teacher education program and were built on the projects and interests of faculty members, (b) modeling appropriate uses of technology in teacher education courses was essential to pre-service teachers' ability to plan K-12 technology-enhanced lessons, and (c) design teams and pre-service teachers reflected about their uses of technology and presented their findings at technology conferences.

Curriculum design teams were organized according to naturally occurring alliances in the teacher education program and were built on the projects and interests of faculty members. Building on these alliances and relations, rather than constructing new ones, allowed for the integration activities to develop quickly. Design team members shared a great deal both personally and professionally. The Inquiry Learning Design Team was organized because of several shared interests, including the intersection of problem-based learning and technology integration and felt that WebQuests provided them with a unique opportunity to collaborate. Although the members of this team were not in the same discipline, they shared a commitment to providing their students with opportunities to integrate technology within the context of problem-based lessons. Working from these common goals, this team has had a significant collaboration experience that will be sustained well beyond the grant's life. Each design team was successful in part because of the common goals they shared with respect to curriculum redesign and technology integration. One design team member said, "In my opinion, the greatest benefit of the PT3 grant has been the sense of community that has been created through it. This has been very important. It has brought people from different programs together and got them talking."

Modeling appropriate uses of technology in teacher education courses was essential to pre-service teachers' ability to write K-12 technology-enhanced lessons. We introduced students to technology-enhanced inquiry learning, problem-based instruction, WebQuest development, and action research assignments before we asked them to write similar lessons. Eula and Marv developed inquiry-based mathematics and science lessons and required research on the Internet. Leigh and Brenda developed WebQuests to introduce science and literacy content. Nancy and Merrell modeled action research and reflection in both portfolio development and curriculum assignments. All three design teams assigned their pre-service teachers to design and evaluate similar inquiry or problem-based, technology-enhanced assignments. An observer from outside of the grant activities said, "The grant has changed the use of technology in the BYU College of Education. It is obvious that there is more emphasis here in the College of Education than anywhere on campus."

Design teams and pre-service teachers reflected about technology integration and presented their findings at technology conferences. Eula shared her newly found enthusiasm for technology practices with Marv after attending the SITE conference at the end of the first year of the grant. They began immediately to plan how to document their own development with technology during the remainder of the grant. Roni Jo's specific role with the Inquiry Learning Design Team was to help them reflect and document their uses of technology and the development of their students' uses of technology. Nancy and Merrell designed instruction around action research both to model technology use and to engage their students with Internet research and technology presentation tools. Merrell stated, "Their action research and applications of technology had importance to themselves and to others. As indicated by the projects completed, the research conducted, the organization and presentation of information and results, and the functional uses of these efforts became evident."

The teacher education program implementing this PT3 grant encouraged inquiry-based instruction in unit planning as part of its restructuring. The unit plans produced by pre-service students in this program supporting research and decision-making are evidence that the PT3 training efforts are having an impact on our pre-service instructors. The results of this study indicate that the pre-service teachers are using innovative instructional practices and higher level thinking skills in the unit plans they write. It also indicates that enhancing units with technology encourages these types of activities in the units developed.

Modeling technology-enhanced curriculum created by design teams and the researching of these activities by both faculty and pre-service teachers created a successful PT3 experience. Strong relationships of support were created that have extended beyond the grant. Teacher education curricula have been permanently restructured. Faculty viewed technology not as a distraction from instruction, but as a part of it. Pre-service teachers experienced, created, and evaluated appropriate technology-enhanced instruction.

REFERENCES

Connell, M., & Johnson, L. (2002). *External evaluators' report of BYU's PT3 grant: Year two, 2001-2002.* Prouo, UT: Unpublished report, Brigham Young University.

Carroll, T. G. (2000). If we didn't have the schools we have today would we build the schools we have today? *Contemporary Issues in Technology and Teacher Education.* Retrieved September 28, 2005, from http://www.citejournal.org/vol1/iss1/currentissues/general/article1.htm

Dede, C. (Ed.). (1998). *Learning with technology.* Alexandria, VA: Jossey-Bass.

Dodge, B. (1998). *WebQuests: A strategy for scaffolding higher level learning.* Retrieved Oct. 27, 2004, from webquest.sdsu.edu/necc98.htm

Jostens Learning Corporation. (1997). *Survey analysis by Global Strategy Group.* San Diego, CA: Author.

Kearsley, G. (1998). Educational technology: A critique. *Education Technology, 38*(2), 47-51.

Pappillion, M. L., & Cellitti, A. (1996) Developmental technology inservice training. *Technology and Teacher Education Annual, 1*(1), 427-430.

Raizen, S., Sellwood, P., Todd, R., & Vickers, M. (1995). *Technology education in the classroom.* San Francisco: Jossey-Bass.

Riedl, J. (1995). *The integrated technology classroom: Building self-reliant learners.* Boston: Allyn & Bacon.

Ritchie, D., & Wilburg, K. (1994). Educational variables influencing technology integration. *Journal of Technology and Teacher Education, 2*(2), 143-153.

doi:10.1300/J025v23n03_08

David Gibson

Elements of Network-Based Assessment

SUMMARY. Elements of network-based assessment systems are envisioned based on recent advances in knowledge and practice in learning theory, assessment design and delivery, and semantic web interoperability. The architecture takes advantage of the mediating role of technology as well as recent models of assessment systems. This overview of the elements outlines the advantages of technology for facilitating new forms of assessment, includes a brief discussion of a contemporary model of assessment design, and is illustrated with a case study of an application of the architecture. The case study is drawn from a research and development technology project (eTIPS) that was funded by the U.S. Department of Education's Preparing Tomorrow's Teachers to Use Technology program. doi:10.1300/J025v23n03_09 *[Article copies available for a fee from The Haworth Document Delivery Service: 1-800-HAWORTH. E-mail address: <docdelivery@haworthpress.com> Website: <http://www.HaworthPress.com> © 2006 by The Haworth Press, Inc. All rights reserved.]*

KEYWORDS. Assessment systems, case-based learning, learning theory, semantic web, information technology, automated assessment, automated essay scoring, network-based assessment

DAVID GIBSON is Founder & President, CurveShift, Stowe, VT 05672 (E-mail: david.gibson@curveshift.com).

[Haworth co-indexing entry note]: "Elements of Network-Based Assessment." Gibson, David. Co-published simultaneously in *Computers in the Schools* (The Haworth Press, Inc.) Vol. 23, No. 3/4, 2006, pp. 131-150; and: *Teaching Teachers to Use Technology* (ed: D. LaMont Johnson, and Kulwadee Kongrith) The Haworth Press, Inc., 2006, pp. 131-150. Single or multiple copies of this article are available for a fee from The Haworth Document Delivery Service [1-800-HAWORTH, 9:00 a.m. - 5:00 p.m. (EST). E-mail address: docdelivery@haworthpress.com].

Assessment, for both the improvement of performance and evaluating learners, is most effective when it reflects learning as "multidimensional, integrated, and revealed in performance over time" (Walvoord & Anderson, 1998). With that in mind, what do networks and new media have to offer that can assist and improve educational assessment? This paper asserts that network-based assessment offers fundamentally new possibilities for knowing what students know.

Networks, as used here, are an integration of the Internet, computers, intranets, and humans offering new forms of instruction and assessment. Network-based assessment is emerging within educational testing and measurement as well as online teaching and learning (Bennet, 1999; Mislevy, Steinberg, & Almond, 2000). In educational testing and measurement, there are examples of large-scale online testing and scoring such as the online SAT and GRE. In online teaching and learning, there are numerous reflective writings, small sample studies of classes, and innovative experiments documented in the Society for Information Technology in Teacher Education (SITE) conference proceedings and journals over the last several years.

A great deal of the literature on online assessment is concerned with design and delivery to students in online courses. These studies primarily offer advice on ways to reproduce face-to-face methods and standards of quality, with some suggestions about ways to use standard telecommunications tools such as e-mail and discussion threads to determine what students know and can do (e.g., Perrin & Mayhew, 2000; Robles & Braathen, 2002; Roblyer & Ekhaml, 2000). Some policy groups underscore the same view of technology as "almost like" face-to-face settings. For example, the first assumption of the American Distance Education Consortium's (http://www.adec.edu/) guiding principles for distance teaching and learning is that "the principles that lend themselves to quality face-to-face learning environments are often similar to those found in web-based environments." The definition of good teaching articulated by the American Association for Higher Education's (http://www.aahe.org/) "Seven Principles of Good Practice in Undergraduate Education" remained the same after being revised for online teaching. We are nevertheless convinced that the new media means more than "almost face-to-face." New media has changed the landscape of teaching, learning, and assessment.

Researchers who agree that the landscape has changed are interested in the unique affordances of network-based teaching and learning, and have begun to articulate a general framework for assessment. For example, some have outlined a broad framework for assessment, from which we can build a new architecture for network-based assessment (Almond, Steinberg, & Mislevy, 2002; Pellegrino, Chudowsky, & Glaser, 2001). Others have begun to outline techniques for estimating the best problem or resource to present to a learner given a set of problems already completed (Almond & Mislevy, 1999; Hawkes & Derry, 1989; Steinberg & Gitomer, 1996). Innovators in the field of latent semantic analysis and applications of Bayesian theory are beginning to show essay scoring results that rival human scoring (McCallum & Nigam, 1998; Rudner & Liang, 2002). Others, using neural net analysis, can categorize the problem-solving approach of learners in a Web-based environment (Stevens, Lopo, & Wang, 1996). These examples begin to point to a qualitatively new role for Internet-based technologies in assessment, one that is rich with multimedia, responsive to learners, flexible over many situations, unobtrusive to the natural actions of learning, and assisted by artificial and network intelligence.

Network-based assessment methods and media have the potential to transform how assessments help us know what students know. The new technology-enhanced conception of assessment stands in contrast to the traditional view of assessments as "tests" of knowledge remembered. Instead, the new perspective on assessment seeks to create a body of "evidence" of usable and available knowledge observed in natural settings of the learner (Greeno, Collins & Resnick, 1997; Mislevy, Steinberg & Almond, 2000). In contrast, some have argued that the fundamental adjustment needed in online assessment is primarily due to a lack of face-to-face contact (O'Malley & McCraw, 1999). Others have pointed to the difficulties of preserving secrecy of items in traditional item response theory tests (Perrin & Mayhew, 2000). But the development of effective and reliable assessments for online students requires a great deal of innovation and departure from traditional practices (Ryan, 2000). Because technology mediates learning in new ways, it engenders new forms of knowledge as well as possibilities for documentation and analysis (Bransford, Brown, & Cocking, 2000; Bruce & Levin, 1997; Greenfield & Cocking, 1996; Kafai, 1995) and should therefore focus our attention on expanding our conceptions of assessment.

What follows is a brief outline of the meditating role of technology and what those new affordances mean for teaching and learning. That discussion is followed by an introduction to the major elements in contemporary designs for assessment systems, and how network-based assessment processes can take advantage of these perspectives. Finally, a case study is presented to illustrate the new elements in use in a network-based assessment system.

TECHNOLOGY AS MEDIATOR IN TEACHING, LEARNING, AND ASSESSMENT

"When used to its full potential, the computer is more than a tool for efficiency and automation: it transforms thinking and creates new knowledge" (Kalik, 2001).

Technology mediates knowledge and thus fundamentally changes learning, teaching, and assessment; what we can know about what students know (Bruce & Levin, 1997). This view contrasts with traditional views of the computer as an automaton, a tool for efficiency in searching, organizing, and communicating knowledge, and a place to store information. The mediating role of technology, extended to network-based assessment, also contrasts with the traditional view of an assessment as providing documentation of what has been learned. In place of these views, the computer combined with global networks is seen as an extension of thinking, inquiry, and expression that transforms the reach and power of the mind. In this section, the claim is made that a new landscape of learning has appeared with network-based technologies and that changed environment is briefly outlined, with implications for network-based assessment.

We begin by considering "the effects of technologies as operating to a large extent through the ways that they alter the environments for thinking, communicating, and acting in the world. Thus, they provide new media for learning, in the sense that one might say land provided new media for creatures to evolve" (Bruce & Levin, 1997, p. 5). A partial listing of the fundamentally new affordances made possible through network-based technologies includes:

1. *Access to an abundant multimedia global knowledge storehouse.* Network-based resources include digital libraries such as the NICI Virtual Library (www.vlibrary.org), real-world data for analysis, and connections to other people who provide information, feedback, and inspiration, all of which can enhance learning and assessment. Furthermore, today's Internet, as vast as it seems, is just the beginning of network-based multimedia, and represents a small fraction of global knowledge available now in digital form, with an even vaster array of information in nondigital form that is quickly finding its way onto the Web. "Deep Web" and "interoperability" methods will soon make available several orders of magnitude more information than is available today. (See the W3C Web site http://www.w3.org/ for

more information on these topics.) In addition, that access is multimedia: involving texts, images, sounds, digital video, and more, which evidence suggests is a rich and effective environment for learning (USDOE, 2000). Design and delivery of multimedia assessment are in their infancy, as is the use of globally linked multimedia resources in network-based assessments.

2. *A vastly expanded range of tools for inquiry and expression.* New network-based media is more than a storage medium for information; it is a new environment for inquiry, expression, construction, and communication. The frontiers of science illustrate this, as they are dominated by new visualization, aural and analytic capabilities that have only become available within the last few years (Novak, 2002). Yet, teaching, learning, and assessment have yet to take full advantage of these developments. Technologies can help users visualize difficult-to-understand concepts—a boon for learners as well as teachers. In assessment for example, that enhanced capability can help teachers see the conceptual growth of the learner or view the structural shape of performance of a group of learners (Stevens, 1991). Learners can work with modeling software similar to the tools used in scientific and work-related environments, which can "increase their conceptual understanding and the likelihood of transfer from school to nonschool settings" (Bruce & Levin, 1997). Most important, the new range of inquiry and expression changes the nature and extent of knowledge and its acquisition. For example, new forms of computational proof and demonstration have opened up branches of mathematics that were considered intractable in the past (Wolfram, 2002), and the role of computational simulation has taken on enlarged importance for the sciences, including cognitive science (Holland, Holyoak, Nisbett, & Thagard, 1986). Additional examples include the use of visualization, simulation, and network-based communities in the discovery of new chemical materials, the human genome project, astronomy and physics. In network-based assessment, the techniques of remote sensing can lead to unobtrusive observations of learners who, rather than taking a test, are making decisions, constructing artifacts, and thinking aloud as they work in a naturally productive setting.

3. *More interactive and responsive applications.* "Because many new technologies are interactive, it is now easier to create environments in which students can learn by doing, receive feedback, and continually refine their understanding and build new

knowledge" (Bransford, Brown, & Cocking, 2000, p. 194). However, thus far much of the development of interactivity has taken place in home-based entertainment and educational games, and those applications are just beginning to tap the potential of network-based technologies–for example, in globally extended massively multi-player online role-playing games (MMORPG, see http://www.mmorpg.com/). In addition, as global network-based interoperability takes hold, new forms of responsive dissemination are emerging (Gibson, Knapp, & Kurowski, 2002) which are making it possible to envision learning environments where the active status of the learner launches a variety of software agents that search the global knowledge store. Agents can return with links to resources and people, and present the next best item for consideration, study, or enjoyment. Thus, the creative impulses of the learner can be met by interactive, multimedia technology that provides new avenues to draw upon a learner's strengths, interests, and aspirations.

4. *New social networks and schools of thought.* The Internet makes unrestricted social networks possible, as well as the possibility that new forms of school and other social organizations may arise in response to the thoughts and actions of groups who share common goals. As network-based technologies become embedded in daily social life, they tend to become invisible; "we focus less on the fact that they may be consciously employed as a tool to do a task, and come to see the task itself as central, with the technology as substrate" (Bruce & Levin, 1997, p. 5). Today for example, some people can contact nearly everyone they work with at anytime via an electronic message system. Yet for all the ways that technologies are becoming an invisible part of our lives, education is still largely organized around traditional face-to-face settings, except in a few "leading edge" projects. Perhaps most importantly, the new social communications systems are interactive, and conducive to active, engaged learning. Network-based assessment systems, for example, are just now emerging that take advantage of social groups (Gibson, 2002). Students can choose what to see and do, and the media can unobtrusively record as well as extend what they learn. Learning can be, more than ever and in ways not possible without networks, driven by the individual needs and interests of the learner in balance with the social goals of education (Friedrichs & Gibson, 2001; Bruce & Levin, 1997).

In addition to these new affordances, network-based assessment systems can also take advantage of recent advances in the science of assessing thinking and learning (Pellegrino, Chudowsky, & Glaser, 2001) including the following:

1. Complex performances can be supported and documented in network-based assessments via multimedia, multileveled, and multiply connected bases of knowledge.
2. With many instances of the learner interacting with applications in different times, places, and contexts, network-based assessments can build a long-term record of documentation, showing how learners change over time.
3. Analysis of expert-novice differences can be facilitated across groups, across space and time, drawing from an evolving common knowledge store.
4. The interactive potential of network-based assessment opens up new possibilities for fostering and determining metacognitive skills of the learner.
5. Emerging capabilities in metadata generation offer the potential for identifying the problem-solving strategies of learners.
6. Unobtrusive observation techniques combined with libraries of evidence and tasks can make possible timely feedback to learners and teachers and matching of current needs with best "next step" materials, tasks, and challenges, including tasks that involve transfer of learning to new contexts.
7. Network-based assessments can include statistical analysis and displays of information to assist learners and teachers in making inferences about performance.

This section briefly outlined eleven ideas that form a set of criteria or an agenda for developing a network-based assessment system: four broad categories that illustrate the mediating potential of network-based technologies, and seven criteria for assessment systems grounded in recent research. The next section outlines two of the potential implications of these elements on teaching, learning, and assessment the potential for developing adaptive expertise in learners, and an expansion of methodologies for assessing the range of knowledge and skill of the learner.

IMPLICATIONS FOR TEACHING, LEARNING, AND ASSESSMENT

Teaching and learning supported by the elements outlined previously can shift from an over-dependence on short-term memory and using procedures, to creative, interdependent, and iterative processes of knowledge construction. Such a shift is necessary in order to deal with massive access to information, essentially limitless bounds for social interactions, and completely novel ways of interacting with and expressing information and ideas. Some commentators have noted this shift as part of a larger movement from an industrially based economy to a knowledge-driven society, bringing with it new demands of flexible and adaptive responses by learners. As Kalik (2001) observed:

> The chief implication of a shift to "knowledge work" is that knowledge workers adapt their responses to a given situation instead of carrying out standard operating procedures. They attempt to understand what would be an appropriate response to a situation, then marshal the necessary resources and capabilities to get it done. They are good problem solvers. (pp. Intro to Section X)

These new demands on learners' thinking are signs of what cognitive scientists call "adaptive expertise" (Bransford, Brown, & Cocking, 2000) which network-based assessments can be designed to measure. In systems designed to develop and measure adaptive expertise, learners are viewed on a continuum with other knowledge workers, including their teachers. Teachers, in turn, who want to be flexible and adaptive themselves, must become curriculum designers who assist learners in planning, marshalling resources and validating that learning has taken place. Assessment methods and reporting has to follow these trends in order to stay well aligned and to measure what is important as well as what is actually taught and learned. Assessment designers thus need to understand and begin with a model of cognition that includes problem-solving, analysis skills, and varying degrees of expertise (Pellegrino, Chudowsky & Glaser, 2001).

The cognitive challenges inherent in problem-solving, analysis, and adaptive expertise are measurable within a performance range that differs for various learners, identified by Vygotsky (1978) as the "zone of proximal development." Increased interactivity and responsiveness of network-based assessments will improve the measurement of the top of the zone. The zone represents the difference between what a learner can do with help and what he or she can do without guidance, and thus has a minimum as well as a maximum that should be measurable by assessments. We can assume that what a learner can do without help or guidance, as is often the case in traditional "test" settings, measures near the bottom of the zone. In network-based assessments, unobtrusive observation and documentation of a learner's explorations, attempts, and responses can add new probes that are closer to the natural context of actions of the learner. And more important, interactive network-based assessments, by providing guidance and new resources during the creation of responses and work products, can measure near the top of the zone, which would represent an advance toward assessments that better assist learners and teachers to achieve maximum performance.

In summary, the previous two sections begin to show that there is a unique new potential for network-based assessments to measure what students and teachers know and can do. The forms of delivery and interactions are dramatically different from traditional assessments, giving rise to new possibilities for forms of collecting and analyzing information that are better aligned with what we know about how people learn. To take advantage of the new potential, researchers and developers can take advantage of a new model for the design and delivery of assessments that can be applied to network-based technologies, including those that combine computers and human expertise.

A NEW MODEL FOR ASSESSMENT DESIGN AND DELIVERY

Recent work has led to a new model of assessment design. Pellegrino, Chudowsky, and Glaser (2001) show that every assessment, regardless of its purpose, involves three fundamental components: "a model of how students represent knowledge and develop competence in the subject domain, tasks or situations that allow one to observe students' performance, and an interpretation method for drawing inferences from the performance evidence thus obtained" (p. 36). In addition to this triadic internal structure, assessments only operate successfully in a context in which learners have been given an opportunity to learn, for example, through curriculum and instruction. The assessment tasks or situations must be aligned with actual opportunities to learn in order to provide good information to any intended audience (learner, teacher, public) for an assessment.

Deepening and extending the three-part model, Almond, Steinberg, and Mislevy (2002) outlined several submodels in the design as well as delivery of assessment systems. Relating their core models to Pellegrino, Chudowsky, and Glaser (2001) and including a brief description, produces an architecture for building network-based assessment systems:

1. *Student model.* A model of how students represent knowledge and develop competence in the subject domain, which specifies the dependencies and statistical properties of relationships among variables that lead to claims about the knowledge, skills, and abilities of the learner. A scoring record holds the values of those variables at a point in time.

2. *Task model.* Tasks or situations that allow one to observe students' performance, which specify variables used to describe key features of tasks (e.g., content, difficulty), the presentation format (e.g., directions, stimulus, prompts), and the work or response product (e.g., answers, work samples). Closely related to the task model is the "presentation model," which specifies how a task will be rendered (e.g., on screen, audio, on hand-held).

3. *Evidence model.* An interpretation method for drawing inferences from the performance evidence thus obtained, which specifies how to identify and evaluate features of the work or response product, and how to update the scoring record.

Almond, Steinberg, and Mislevy (2002) describe the following two submodels that fall outside of the Pellegrino, Chudowsky and Glaser (2001) model, since these submodels deal more with construction and delivery than design (Figure 1).

4. *Assembly model.* Methods for assembling and delivering assessments, which specify how an assessment will be assembled (e.g., iterative and interactive as online, redundant and complete as on paper).

5. *Delivery model.* A catch-all container for all of the above models and includes constraints that do not fit elsewhere (e.g., security, backup, administration control)

The network-based system illustrated by the case study in the following section extends this model of assessment to include a globally shared library of resources behind each submodel. As the new assessment architecture becomes a common vocabulary among assessment designers, the possibility increases for sharing that vocabulary and structure as a Web-based ontology for searching and finding assessment objects. Utilizing XML and RDF schema (Knapp, Kurowski, Dexter, Gibson, & McLaughlin, 2004), researchers are beginning to develop interoperable systems that allow the creation of a wide variety of locally relevant assessments from globally available resources. The essential

FIGURE 1. A model for design and delivery of assessment systems, adapted from Almond, Steinberg, & Mislevy (2002).

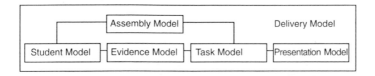

tools and approaches of the architecture have been developing within the global "World Wide Web Consortium" (W3C) (http://www.w3.org/) which develops interoperable technologies, specifications, guidelines, software, and tools to lead the World Wide Web to its full potential. W3C is a forum for information, commerce, communication, and collective understanding.

With a general model of an assessment system available and the mediating potential outlined above, we next turn to case study examples to illustrate the new elements of network-based assessment.

CASE STUDY EXAMPLES

The eTIP Cases project, funded by the U.S. Department of Education's Preparing Tomorrow's Teachers to Use Technology–Catalyst program (ETIPs, 2002), has built a number of online simulations intended for pre-service teacher education programs. The simulations are set in the context of imitation Web sites for several different schools, and provide online, multimedia case, based instruction and assessment that can help pre-service teachers and teacher education faculty learn about effective integration and successful implementation of educational technology.

The content of the Educational Technology Integration and Implementation Principles, or eTIPs cases, draws from the National Educational Technology Standards (NETS, 2002), the Interstate New Teacher Assessment and Support Consortium (INTASC, 2002) standards, and the National Staff Development Council (NSDC, 2002) standards for staff development programs as well as the experience of the case writers. A matrix of "sim-schools" has been created in which rural, suburban and urban settings were crossed with high-performing, mid-performing, and low-performing student results and staff development data. This produced a rich simulation context of schools in which questions of technology innovation, teacher preparation, and staff development can be raised.

Each question creates a new "case." Several cases are brought together into a "problem set," and several problem sets can exist within one over-arching "problem space" created by the matrix of school types and characteristics. The flexibility and reusability of the major elements–cases, sets, and spaces–form the heart of the task model of the network-based assessment system. Two items contribute to the definition of each case within a problem set: the prologue, which sets out the challenge or situation and requests a student work product or response, and a table of weights that determines the relevancy of the description items for a particular prologue. The relevancy table is used in the analysis of the resources learners use while constructing their responses, and thus functions as an idealized student model, detailing how an expert learner would view the relevancy of the contents in the site concerning the question at hand.

The presentation model for each case includes a unique prologue that frames the challenge or situation and calls for the learner to make a decision and produce response. Then, through a menu of hyperlinks, learners explore the range of information available to use in developing their response to the challenge. Context-rich descriptions of classroom and school settings are presented in text, visual, and audio formats. The multimedia elements and descriptions, which are also items or data variables for the assessment analysis in the evidence model, can be selected in any sequence. The hyperlinked items, the scenario posed, and the case's weighted contents constitute a specific problem space context through which learners navigate as they construct their response. Responses can be either machine or human scored, including remote scoring by social networks of peers and experts. While the overall approach is constructivist, each case is not so open-ended and complex as to overwhelm the user (Mayer, 1997).

To illustrate, "H. Usher Elementary School" is one of the simulated schools set in an urban location. It is a medium-size school, with about 700 students. Although the learners don't know it when first encountering the simulation, H. Usher is a high performing school, yet according to the prologue, its faculty and administration perceives that it has a problem with student results. The prologue to the simulation states that the second grade students are not meeting the district goals and need to advance their reading comprehension at a faster pace. The learner is challenged to explore the school context to understand more about the learning environment in which this situation has occurred, decide what went wrong, and write a response explaining what to do differently as a second-grade teacher given the resources that are available. In this case, as learners try to figure out how this school works, they find evidence of a high-performing staff development program and a school that outperforms the district and state. How will inexperienced future teachers view this situation calling for a complex performance (deciding what information is relevant and not, deciding what options might work in this setting, writing about their decision and justifying it)? The eTIP Cases project is designed to help pre-service educators and future teachers find out.

Problem spaces like H. Usher contain many potential challenges or situations and solution paths. The content of the school's Web site contains an abundance of rich information that allows several prologues to be created. Each prologue can ask different meaningful questions, such as questions about technology integration in the fourth grade, the principal's attitude toward peer support systems, the state of professional development, the needs of students given their performance on state assessments, and so on. This allows a single problem space to function as a generic task and presentation model over many "cases" and "problem sets."

VISUALIZING AND ANALYZING PROBLEM SOLVING

As the learner navigates around the problem space, reading, watching, and listening to the items, the application tracks the sequence and timing of items used and collects the learner's response product in the form of essays, which can be scored by the teacher and others. By tracking the learner's use of items, the application creates a performance record as part of the evidence model that documents the development of learner-reasoned relationships among problem space variables. In addition to the performance record, which is captured as an unobtrusive observation, a work product in the form of an essay is gathered. The narrative of the essay stores information directly from learners concerning their decisions, rationale, and what was meaningful in their analysis.

Inspiration for the eTIPs application came from the IMMEX (2002) system, developed first for chemistry and the physical sciences, and extended by CurveShift (VI, 2002) to include an essay scoring capability and an online campus to help introduce new teacher education faculty to the process of using the cases. IMMEX provides timely feedback to learners and teachers through a number of quantitative displays of the performance records of users, including visual displays called "search path maps" (Stevens, 1991). In these maps, each student action is represented by a rectangle that is colored to visually relate items closely linked by content, concepts, or type within the content domains in the problem space. These icons are organized in different configurations and lines connect the sequences of items selected by the students while performing the case (Figure 2).

Teachers can use these maps in multiple ways. For teacher educators the maps provide a validity check on their classroom preparation and emphasis as well as a source of information about student performance differences. By comparing earlier to later maps, one can determine a learner's progress over time through refinements of problem-solving approaches. Providing students with their own maps encourages reflection, which can be combined with in-class discussion and writing. Search path maps are particularly important for examining and promoting the metacognitive aspects of problem-solving such as persistence, elimination of alternative hypotheses, efficiency, confidence, and certainty. The maps also supply artifacts for developing problem-solving scoring rubrics and for discovery of problem-solving strategy patterns across groups of performances, including by artificial neural network analysis (Kanowith-Klein, Stave, Stevens, & Casillas, 2001), an approach that helps automate the interpretation process through pattern recognition.

CurveShift enhancements to IMMEX added essay scoring to the feedback available to the learner. Essays offer a way to enhance the metacognitive skills of students. The application supports the creation of scoring rubrics (Table 1), which have been used by the eTIPs project to create six rubrics, one for each eTIP. The rubrics are viewable and printable by teachers, and can be used to guide essay writing. An essay grading form is provided to record essay scores (Figure 3) and reports can be generated that compare performances across several essays in a problem set. Essays scores can be compared with search path map information (e.g., by comparing the justification of a decision with the knowledge domains visited during the search for information).

Also, with relevancy scores available for each item in the problem space, a score can be created that relates the efficiency of searches with the scores on the essay. An overall relevancy score is computed that relates the total items visited to the sum of the level of relevancy of the items. A high relevancy score with a ratio to all searches that approaches "2" (meaning that all items searched were highly relevant)

FIGURE 2. Sample student search path maps. *Note:* The first map represents a student who explored many menu items, making a complete search of the problem space. The performance of the student in the second map shows that only two general areas of the problem space were explored, indicating a lack of grasp of the concepts underlying the problem. Taken from eTIPs documentation.

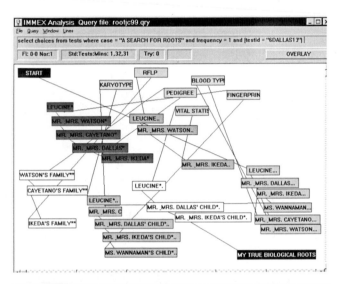

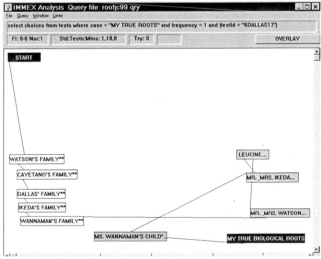

TABLE 1. Sample eTIP Rubric

Criteria	Level 1	Level 2	Level 3
1. Validation: Explains the central classroom challenge in the case.	Does not present an explanation of instructional planning in relation to curriculum goals or standards.	Presents a limited explanation of instructional planning in relation to curriculum goals or standards.	Articulates a clear explanation of instructional planning in relation to curriculum goals or standards.
2. Evidence: Identifies case information that must be considered in a decision about using technology aligned with curriculum goals or standards.	Does not identify aspects of case information, including appropriate technology uses, that aligns with curriculum goals or standards.	Identifies aspects of case information, including appropriate technology uses, without explanation or examples of how these align with curriculum goals or standards.	Identifies aspects of case information, including appropriate technology uses, with explanation or examples of how these align with curriculum goals or standards.
3. Decision: States a justified recommendation for implementing a viable classroom option to address the challenge.	Does not state a recommendation for using, or not using, a particular technology in the curriculum.	Presents a limited recommendation for using, or not using, a particular technology in the curriculum.	Presents a well-justified recommendation for using, or not using, a particular technology in the curriculum.

Note: The rubric maker can accommodate any number of criteria and score points.

FIGURE 3. Sample essay score using the Essay Grading Tool. Note: Total score and average score are computed based on the rubric scores for each criteria as well as a global score.

In his/her own words (200-300), the credential candidate's essay clearly demonstrates his/her decision-making process about using technology to meet a range of learning needs of the diverse group of students in the case.			
Criteria:	Level 0	Level 1	Level 2
1. Validation: Explains the **central classroom challenge** in the case			X
2. Evidence: Identifies **case information** that must be considered in a decision about using technology to differentiate instruction to meet the diverse needs of learners		X	
3. Decision: States a **justified recommendation** for implementing a viable classroom option to address the challenge		X	

Global Score:
Does Not Meet Expectation because Decision score above = 0
Does Not Meet Expectation because both Validation and Evidence score above = 0
Meets Expectation because scores in both Decision/Validation or Decision/Evidence = 2
Exemplary because scores for all three criteria (Validation/Evidence/Decision) = 2
✓**Somewhat Meets Expectation because your scores meet none of the above rules**
Global score not available.

Narrative Evaluation:
Test of the system...with new ruibric scorer.

might represent an expert score, that can be used in an analysis of expert-novice differences. Changes in performance over time can also be used to show those differences.

At present, the evidence model of the eTIP Cases is in an early stage; thus, there is still much to learn about computing relevancy, relating that to score profiles on essays, and comparing that with search path map data. However, it is clear that there is potential for documenting complex performances that involve problem solving, analysis, and metacognition.

THE FUTURE OF NETWORK-BASED ASSESSMENT

The future of network-based assessment will take advantage of WorldWide Web architecture, the Semantic Web, for inoperability of systems. The Semantic Web (Berners-Lee, Hendler, & Lassila, 2001) allows applications to share data, even if they were built independently and remotely from one another. For example, the eTIPs instruction and assessment application on IMMEX in California sends essays to Colorado where they are picked up and scored by people in Vermont, using the CurveShift essay scoring tool, and then returned to a classroom for display to the teacher, who may be in Minnesota. The future of network-based assessments seems headed toward such distributed systems.

Semantic Web applications will enable building digital catalogs of resources that take advantage of a decentralized network of experts, such as the scorers in Vermont adding information to a classroom in Minnesota. Intelligent routing of those resources can then respond to queries that express the essay score, a multidimensional score from a survey, and other profiles of a user's strengths, interests, and aspirations. Human advisors and teachers can utilize new forms of network-based assessment to provide guidance to learners and validation of learning, resulting in highly personalized instruction, guidance, and assessment applications.

As network-based assessment systems are developing, they will be guided by new conceptions of teaching, learning, and assessment, where teaching is seen as a guiding activity for planning, marshaling resources, and validating learning; learning is seen as a process of developing patterns and procedures to acquire and use knowledge in social and technological settings; and assessment is seen as an unobtrusive network-based activity that produces a rich record for analysis and making inferences about learners.

REFERENCES

Almond, R., & Mislevy, R. (1999). Graphical models and computerized adaptive testing. *Psychological Measurement, 23*, 223-237.

Almond, R., Steinberg, L., & Mislevy, R. (2002, October). Enhancing the design and delivery of assessment systems: A four process architecture. *The Journal of Technology, Learning, and Assessment, 1*, 5.

Bennet, R. (1999). Using new technology to improve assessment. *Educational Measurement: Issues and Practice, 18*, 5-12.

Berners-Lee, T., Hendler, J., & Lassila, O. (2001). The Semantic Web: A new form of Web content that is meaningful to computers will unleash a revolution of new possibilities. *Scientific American, 284*, 5, 34-43.

Bransford, J., Brown, A. & Cocking, R. (2000). *How people learn: Brain, mind, experience and school.* Washington: DC. National Academy Press.

Bruce, B., & Levin, J. (1997). Educational technology: Media for inquiry, communication, construction, and expression. *Journal of Educational Computing Research, 17*,1, 79-102.

ETIPs. (2002). Available at http://www.etips.info/

Friedrichs, A., & Gibson, D. (2001). Personalization and secondary school renewal. In *Personal learning: Preparing high school students to create their future* (pp. 41-68). A. DiMartino & J. Clarke, (Eds.), Lanham, Maryland: Scarecrow Press.

Gibson, D. (2002). Functions of an online mentoring and professional learning portal. Paper presented at the 2003 EdMedia conference. Montreal, Quebec.

Gibson, D., Knapp, M., & Kurowski, B. (2002). *Building responsive dissemination systems for education with the Semantic Web: Using the new open-source "liber" application.* Paper presented at the 2003 EdMedia conference, Montreal, Quebec.

Greenfield, P., & Cocking, R. (Eds.) (1996). *Interacting with video.* Greenwich, CT: Abbex.

Greeno, J. G., Collins, A. M., & Resnick, L. B. (1996). Cognition and learning. In D.C. Berliner and R.C. Calfee (Eds.), *Handbook of Educational Psychology* (pp. 15-45). NY: Simon & Schuster Macmillan.

Hawkes, L., & Derry, S. (1989). Error diagnosis and fuzzy reasoning techniques for intelligent tutoring systems. *Journal of AI in Education, 1*, 43-56.

Holland, J., Holyoak, K., Nisbett, R., & Thagard, P. (1986). *Induction: Processes of inference, learning, and discovery.* Cambridge, MA: MIT Press.

INTASC. (2002). Retrieved April 25, 2006 from http://www.ccsso.org/intasc.html

IMMEX. (2002). Retrieved April 25, 2006 from http://www.immex.ucla.edu/

Kafai, Y. (1995). *Minds in play: Computer game design as a context for children's learning.* Hillsdale, NJ: L. Erlbaum.

Kanowith-Klein, S., Stave, M., Stevens, R., & Casillas, A. (2001). Problem-solving skills among pre-college students in clinical immunology and microbiology: Classifying strategies with a rubric and artificial neural network technology. *Microbiology Education, 2*, 1, 25-33.

Kalik, B. (2001). Teaching thinking through technology: Introduction to Section X. In *Developing minds: A resource book for teaching thinking*, (3rd ed.). A. L. Costa (Ed.), Alexandria,VA: Association for Supervision & Curriculum Development.

Knapp, M., Kurowski, B., Dexter, S., Gibson, D., & McLaughlin, B. (2004). *Metadata co-development: A process resulting in metadata about technical assistance to educators.* Paper presented at the W3C 2003, NYC.

Mayer, R.E. (1997). Multimedia learning: Are we asking the right questions? *Educational Psychologist, 32*, 1-19.

McCallum, A., & Nigam, K. (1998). *A comparison of event models for Naive Bayes text classification.* Paper presented at the American Association for Artificial Intelligence-1998 Workshop on Learning for Text Categorization.

Mislevy, R., Steinberg, L., & Almond, R. (2000). *Leverage points for improving educational assessment.* Paper prepared for an invitational meeting, The Effectiveness of Educational Technology: Research Design for the Next Decade: Menlo Park, CA: SRI International.

National Educational Technology Standards. (2002). Retrieved April 11, 2006, from http://cnets.iste.org

Novak, M. (2002). Presentation at the PT3 Catalyst special conference held in Washington, DC, on November 18-19. Meeting notes.

National Staff Development Council. (2002). Retrieved April 11, 2006, from http://www.nsdc.org/educatorindex.htm

O'Malley, J., & McCraw, H. (1999, Winter). Students perceptions of distance learning, online learning and the traditional classroom. *Online Journal of Distance Learning Administration, 2*(4): Retrieved September 15, 2001, from http://www.westga.edu/distance/omalley24.html

Pellegrino, J., Chudowsky, N., & Glaser, R. (2001). *Knowing what students know: The science and design of educational assessment.* Washington, DC: National Academy Press.

Perrin, K. M., & Mayhew, D. (2000). The reality of designing and implementing an Internet-based course. *Online Journal of Distance Learning Administration, 3*(4). Retrieved September 15, 2001, from http://www.westga.edu/distance/ojdla/winter34/mayhew34.html

Robles, M., & Braathen, S. (2002). Online assessment techniques. *Delta Pi Epsilon Journal, 44* (1), 39-49.

Roblyer, M. D., & Ekhaml, L. (2000). How interactive are YOUR distance courses? A rubric for assessing interaction in distance learning. *Online Journal of Distance Learning Administration, 3*(2). Retrieved September 15, 2001, from http://www.westga.edu/distance/roblyer32.html

Rudner, L., & Liang, T. (2002, April 1-5). *Automated essay scoring using Baye's theorem.* Paper presented at the annual meeting of the National Council on Measurement in Education, New Orleans, LA.

Ryan, R. C. (2000). Student assessment comparison of lecture and online construction equipment and methods classes. *THE Journal, 27*(6), 78-83.

Steinberg, L., & Gitomer, D. (1996). Intelligent tutoring and assessment built on an understanding of a technical problem-solving task. *Instructional Science, 24,* 223-258.

Stevens, R. (1991). Search path mapping: A versatile approach for visualizing problem-solving behavior. *Academic Medicine, 66,* 9, S72-S75.

Stevens, R., Lopo, A., & Wang, P. (1996). Artificial neural networks can distinguish novice and expert strategies during complex problem solving. *Journal of the American Medical Informatics Association, 3,* 131-138.

United States Department of Education. (2000). *Two exemplary and five from promising educational technology programs.* Retrieved April 11, 2006, from http://www.ed.gov/offices/OERI/ORAD/LTD/newtech_progs.html

Vermont Institutes. (2002). Retrieved April 11, 2006, from http://www.vermontinstitutes.org/

Vygotsky, L. S. (1978). *Mind in society: The development of higher psychological processes.* Cambridge, MA: Harvard University Press.

Walvoord, B.E., & Anderson, V. J. (1998). *Effective grading: A tool for learning and assessment.* San Francisco: Jossey-Bass.

Wolfram, S. (2002). *A new kind of science.* Champaign, IL: Wolfram Media.

doi:10.1300/J025v23n03_09

Cleborne D. Maddux

PT3 and the Deans' Grants:
Some Important Differences

SUMMARY. PT3 and the Deans' Grants of the 1980s have much in common. Both were intended to stimulate the infusion of new material into general teacher education courses. PT3 was aimed at furthering the integration of technology in teacher education, while the Deans' Grants attempted to infuse knowledge and skills related to teaching students with disabilities. The Deans' Grants succeeded in the short term, but failed in the long term, since many general teacher education instructors gradually removed material about disabilities from their course syllabi once the Deans' Grants concluded. PT3 is unlikely to suffer the same long-term fate, due to the seductive nature of technology, which tends to make interest in it self-sustaining. doi:10.1300/J025v23n03_10 *[Article copies available for a fee from The Haworth Document Delivery Service: 1-800-HAWORTH. E-mail address: <docdelivery@haworthpress.com> Website: <http://www.HaworthPress.com> © 2006 by The Haworth Press, Inc. All rights reserved.]*

KEYWORDS. PT3, Deans' Grants, technology in education, special education, teacher education, infusion

CLEBORNE D. MADDUX is Associate Editor for Research, *Computers in the Schools*, and Foundation Professor, Department of Counseling and Educational Psychology, University of Nevada, Reno, Reno, NV 89557 (E-mail: maddux@unr.edu).

[Haworth co-indexing entry note]: "PT3 and the Deans' Grants: Some Important Differences." Maddux, Cleborne D. Co-published simultaneously in *Computers in the Schools* (The Haworth Press, Inc.) Vol. 23, No. 3/4, 2006, pp. 151-155; and: *Teaching Teachers to Use Technology* (ed: D. LaMont Johnson, and Kulwadee Kongrith) The Haworth Press, Inc., 2006, pp. 151-155. Single or multiple copies of this article are available for a fee from The Haworth Document Delivery Service [1-800-HAWORTH, 9:00 a.m. - 5:00 p.m. (EST). E-mail address: docdelivery@haworthpress.com].

New inventions can and will be made; however, nothing new can be thought of that concerns mortal man. Everything has already been thought and said which at best we can express in different forms and give new expressions to.

–Johann Wolfgang Von Goethe (1749-1832),
Conversation with Joseph Sebastian Grüner (August 24, 1823)
(The Columbia World of Quotations, 1996)

Goethe was neither the first nor the last to suggest that there is nothing new under the sun. Perhaps it is true that everything has already been thought and said. Certainly, education in general, and information technology in education in particular have seen their share of old wine in new bottles, an observation brought to mind by this volume. As almost everyone must know by now, the PT3 grants are competitive federal grants dedicated to increasing the speed and quality with which technology is being integrated into teacher education.

The idea of a government grant program aimed at changing the content of teacher education has a familiar ring. Those of us who were faculty members in colleges of education during the late 1970s and early 1980s will be reminded of the *Deans' Grants*. The Deans' Grants were part of a program sponsored by the Office of Special Education to integrate ("infuse" was the politically correct term, at the time) special education methods into the curriculum required for all teachers. These grants, totaling millions of dollars, were made to 260 recipients, primarily deans in colleges of education.

Unfortunately, the program was not a resounding success. A great deal of short-term progress occurred, as noted by the addition of special education topics to the syllabi for many general education courses in institutions that received Deans' Grants. Somewhat predictably, however, when funding from the Deans' Grants ended, regular education professors gradually (or suddenly) deleted knowledge and skills about children with disabilities from their course syllabi.

At first glance, PT3 seems in danger of suffering the same fate as the Deans' Grants. Like the Dean's Grants, short-term success is obvious. As a direct result of the PT3 program, there are many general teacher education faculty members who are, for the first time, intensely interested in integrating technology in their courses. The trend is undeniable. In the last few years, these general education faculty members have begun to inundate conferences dedicated to technology in education. For example, at a recent conference of the Society for Technology in

Teacher Education, I caught sight of the most unlikely of attendees–a department chairperson at an institution at which I used to be a faculty member.

My most vivid memory of this person goes back to a meeting in the 1980s at which I was making a pitch for the then-outlandish idea that the university should provide personal computers for all faculty. This chairperson made an impassioned speech in opposition to this idea, maintaining that secretaries should be doing the "typing" for faculty, and arguing that she would never want a computer in her office because every time she passed my office I was seated in front of it "doing a secretary's work." There she was, without a trace of shame, spending PT3 money to attend a conference on the use of technology in teacher education.

For a moment, I was appalled at her attendance, and at the fact that there were many others at the conference who had never before expressed the slightest interest in technology. "Where were they," I peevishly thought, "when I was struggling with cassette drives on the old Radio Shack Model I, or talking a blue streak to get some administrator to turn loose the money to buy a little software, or stringing cable in a broom closet to connect a daisy-wheel printer for the faculty to share?" "Isn't it strange," I thought sarcastically, "how their interest in technology and the acquisition of PT3 money in their institutions just happened to coincide?"

Almost as soon as I had these thoughts, I realized how illogical they were. Far from resenting new-found interest, I should be celebrating it. These were the very people PT3 was intended to serve! The fact that technology neophytes (and a few Luddites) were at the conference was an indication that PT3 was succeeding. No special funding was needed to ensure the interest of typical attendees at this or any other conference dealing with information technology in education. It was the previously uninterested faculty member such as the chairperson mentioned who thought using a computer was simply typing, who needed some nudging in the direction of technology. Obviously, she and many others were getting the stimulation they needed, as shown by their attendance at the conference, and by the many presentations showing how PT3 has resulted in the integration of technology into general teacher education courses.

So, from an anecdotal standpoint, the short-term success of PT3 seems clear. More formal evaluation results that I have seen are likewise positive. Like the Deans' Grants, however, the proof of the pudding will only become obvious after PT3 funding is gone. The critical question is whether or not these technology neophytes will stop integrating technology into their teacher education courses at that point.

I am cautiously optimistic that such will not be the case. There are major differences between the Deans' Grants and PT3. The Deans' Grant program was aimed at influencing faculty members to include information about disabilities in their regular education courses. This increased the number of topics to be covered in such classes, and required these faculty members to omit something to make room for the new material. Most importantly, the material on disabilities is not so inherently interesting to most students as is technology, and is not capable of streamlining faculty members' day-to-day work. Then, too, there was little, if any incentive for teacher education faculty members to stay abreast of new knowledge and skills related to teaching students with disabilities after the grant ended.

Technology, on the other hand, has much in common with the act of reading. Reading is itself so reinforcing that once it begins to be mastered, further progress becomes almost completely self-sustaining. It would be nearly impossible for anyone who experienced initial success to stop reading. For most people, the same is true of technology. The deeper the mastery of technology, the more personally useful it becomes and the more self-sustaining the interest in technology and in further deepening one's technology skills. Furthermore, unlike the material on disabilities, teachers-in-training generally have a good attitude toward technology, since most are already aware of its utility for word processing and other, similar applications. Therefore, most are highly motivated to follow the instructor's lead and begin to use technology in instruction. Then, too, teachers-in-training are quick to realize that technology makes teaching more effective and more fun, and that it can make new and better ways of teaching and learning available to everyone in their classes.

For these reasons, I believe that PT3 will not suffer the same fate as that which befell the Deans' Grants. A few general education instructors may not sustain their interest in technology, but technology is simply so seductive, and is so ubiquitous in the culture at large, that this will not be a widespread problem. I have never known anyone who willingly gave up e-mail, or who completely stopped surfing the Web. Technology is so inherently interesting and so sweepingly useful that continued use is nearly self-sustaining once one passes a critical point in the learning curve. I believe that PT3 has been responsible for moving most teacher education faculty members who were involved past that critical point.

Some future follow-up research in institutions that housed PT3 grants is needed to determine if the short-term gains experienced from the grants hold up over the next decade and beyond. I invite reports of such research to be submitted for publication in *Computers in the Schools*.

REFERENCE

The columbia world of quotations. (1996). NY: Columbia University Press. Retrieved May 19, 2003 from http://www.bartleby.com/66/17/25217.html

doi:10.1300/J025v23n03_10

Index

BOOK ORDER FORM!

Order a copy of this book with this form or online at:
http://www.HaworthPress.com/store/product.asp?sku= 5970

Teaching Teachers to Use Technology

—— in softbound at $26.00 ISBN-13: 978-0-7890-3504-2 / ISBN-10: 0-7890-3504-9.
—— in hardbound at $60.00 ISBN-13: 978-0-7890-3503-5 / ISBN-10: 0-7890-3503-0.

COST OF BOOKS _____

POSTAGE & HANDLING _____
US: $4.00 for first book & $1.50
for each additional book
Outside US: $5.00 for first book
& $2.00 for each additional book.

SUBTOTAL _____

In Canada: add 6% GST. _____

STATE TAX _____
CA, IL, IN, MN, NJ, NY, OH, PA & SD residents
please add appropriate local sales tax.

FINAL TOTAL _____
If paying in Canadian funds, convert
using the current exchange rate,
UNESCO coupons welcome.

❑ **BILL ME LATER:**
Bill-me option is good on US/Canada/
Mexico orders only; not good to jobbers,
wholesalers, or subscription agencies.

❑ **Signature** _____

❑ **Payment Enclosed: $** _____

❑ **PLEASE CHARGE TO MY CREDIT CARD:**

❑ Visa ❑ MasterCard ❑ AmEx ❑ Discover
❑ Diner's Club ❑ Eurocard ❑ JCB

Account # _____

Exp Date _____

Signature _____
(Prices in US dollars and subject to change without notice.)

PLEASE PRINT ALL INFORMATION OR ATTACH YOUR BUSINESS CARD

Name

Address

City   State/Province   Zip/Postal Code

Country

Tel   Fax

E-Mail

May we use your e-mail address for confirmations and other types of information? ❑Yes ❑No We appreciate receiving
your e-mail address. Haworth would like to e-mail special discount offers to you, as a preferred customer.
We will never share, rent, or exchange your e-mail address. We regard such actions as an invasion of your privacy.

Order from your **local bookstore** or directly from
The Haworth Press, Inc. 10 Alice Street, Binghamton, New York 13904-1580 • USA
Call our toll-free number (1-800-429-6784) / Outside US/Canada: (607) 722-5857
Fax: 1-800-895-0582 / Outside US/Canada: (607) 771-0012
E-mail your order to us: orders@HaworthPress.com

For orders outside US and Canada, you may wish to order through your local
sales representative, distributor, or bookseller.
For information, see http://HaworthPress.com/distributors

(Discounts are available for individual orders in US and Canada only, not booksellers/distributors.)

Please photocopy this form for your personal use.
www.HaworthPress.com

BOF07